Conversations with Myself

Conversations with Myself

100 Stories of Hope, Faith, and Love

VOLUME 1
2nd Edition

HELEN BROWN

Reading Stones Publishing

Copyright © 2020 by Helen Brown.

ISBN: Softcover: 978-0-6488938-0-6
        eBook: 978-0-6488938-1-3

All rights reserved. No part of this book may be reproduced or transmitted in any form or by any means, electronic or mechanical, including photocopying, recording, or by any information storage and retrieval system, without permission in writing from the copyright owner.

Scripture quotations marked KJV are from the Holy Bible, King James Version (Authorized Version). First published in 1611. Quoted from the KJV Classic Reference Bible, Copyright © 1983 by The Zondervan Corporation.

Scripture quotations marked WEB are from the Holy Bible, World English Bible obtained from www.biblegateway.com

Any people depicted in stock imagery provided by Shutterstock are models, and such images are being used for illustrative purposes only.
www.shutterstock.com

Front cover photography and design: Jennifer Maybury < Carpe Noctem Photography>

Published by: Reading Stones Publishing
Helen Brown and Wendy Wood
hbrown1956@gmail.com
woodwendy1982.wixsite.com/readingstones

To order additional copies of this book contact the publisher at:
Glenburnie homestead
212 Glenburnie Rd
Rob Roy NSW 2360
hbrown1956@gmail.com

Contents

1.	A Cup of...	1
2.	Anger	2
3.	Animal	3
4.	Attention Please	4
5.	Bedside	5
6.	Being Content	6
7.	Borrowed	8
8.	Christmas Night	9
9.	Closed Door	11
10.	Clouds	12
11.	Colour	13
12.	Dark	14
13.	Depth of Field	15
14.	Details	16
15.	Dinner	17
16.	Drink	18
17.	Eight O'clock	19
18.	Energy	20
19.	Faceless Self-portrait	21
20.	Fake	22
21.	Favourite	23
22.	Fear	24
23.	Flash or Dash	25
24.	Floral	26
25.	Food	27
26.	Forgotten	28
27.	Four O'clock	29
28.	Free	30
29.	From Where I Stand	31
30.	Frozen Water	32
31.	Fruit to Sauce	33

32.	Get Moving	34
33.	God Sees You	35
34.	God Sings – Psalm 95:1-7.	36
35.	Gone Fishing	37
36.	Grow	39
37.	Ha Ha Ha	40
38.	Hands	41
39.	Happy Place	42
40.	I bought this	43
41.	I bought this on a Sunday!	44
42.	I found this…	45
43.	I Hear	46
44.	I Never	47
45.	In the Air	48
46.	JOY	49
47.	Lighting	50
48.	Looking In	51
49.	Lucky Number	52
50.	Making Mistakes	53
51.	Me Today	54
52.	Nature	55
53.	New	56
54.	Nine O'clock	57
55.	Old Plus New	58
56.	On the Wall	59
57.	Overwhelmed	60
58.	Path	61
59.	Pink	62
60.	Pointy	63
61.	Restore	64
62.	Rings	65
63.	Scrambled Eggs	66
64.	Season	68
65.	Skyline	69
66.	Snack	70
67.	So, this happened!	71
68.	Something Green	72
69.	Something White	73
70.	Sparrows	74

71.	Starts with Rope	75
72.	Starts with "S"	76
73.	Starts with "T"	77
74.	Strange	78
75.	Stripes	79
76.	Summer/Winter	80
77.	Sun	81
78.	Super Results	82
79.	Superannuation	83
80.	Sweet	84
81.	Teaching Myself	85
82.	Testing, Testing, Can You Trust Me?	86
83.	This is Good	87
84.	This Smells so Good	88
85.	Three Things	89
86.	'Tis the Season to	90
87.	Today I Saw...	91
88.	Too Much	92
89.	Tradition	93
90.	Trash	94
91.	Treasure	95
92.	Trivialising Job	96
93.	Twisted and Toughened	98
94.	UP	99
95.	Upside-Down	100
96.	Want	101
97.	Weather	102
98.	Weekends	103
99.	What I wish for	104
100.	What I'm Doing Now	105

1. A Cup of...

Tea, it has to be said, is my favourite drink. It was one of the few things that I could continue to drink after I was diagnosed as a diabetic. I prefer to drink my tea in a mug rather than a cup because mugs seem to hold more tea. I have a variety of mugs in my cupboard. One that was bought for me by my son says: "Now Panic and Freak Out". I'm often accused of doing this, but I would argue against it. Yes, I have been known to raise my voice but like many people say it is to me a form of motivational speaking to my children. How else will they understand the urgency of a situation until my tone changes? I'm not saying that I have never sinned in this process.

The mug does serve as a reverse psychology prompt though. It reminds me that it is a stupid thing to do and a great waste of time. It is a very interesting way of reminding me that God is in control of my life. He has a plan for it, and He has an answer for any problem that I could face. *"For I know the thoughts that I think toward you, saith the LORD, thoughts of peace, and not of evil, to give you an expected end."* Jeremiah 29:11.

There have been many times when I have felt that I was not going to be able to cope. I thank the Lord each day that I was able to ring my mother on many occasions for common-sense advice. I can no longer do that so a mug of tea and a quiet word with the Lord is my new method of reminding myself that He is in control.

2. Anger

A black computer screen brings my anger close to the surface, particularly when the computer has decided to turn itself off while I'm in the middle of typing a story. Because I haven't had any warning, it usually means that when things restart, I have to try and remember what I have typed before, and yes, I'm getting old enough for that to be a little difficult at times.

Yes, it is silly to get angry over such a small thing. There are many things that are more important than a black screen; including times when people are being treated badly and when corruption seems to win over honest dealings.

I will say that while this problem with my computer does make me angry, knowing that it will one day be fixed helps me not to behave badly. If I didn't have this hope I admit that I might find it more difficult to stay calm. *"Be ye angry, and sin not: let not the sun go down upon your wrath:"* Ephesians 4:26.

We see a lot of people acting out their anger these days. We may ask why people are so angry and why they need to take their anger out on others. My guess is, that in many cases, they do not see any way of fixing what it is that makes them angry to begin with.

That is the hope that we have as Christians. No matter what it is that makes us angry we know that one-day God will fix it, on that day when Jesus returns. He will create a new perfect Heaven and Earth and no one will be angry anymore.

3. Animal

I am not an "animal person" which means that I would be quite happy to never have a domestic animal in my life. I am content to let God's wild creatures roam and do what He created them for, as long as they don't invade my personal space. This is not to say that I don't get very upset when those who choose to have animals fail to meet their responsibilities. I even accepted gifts of pets for my children with the aim of teaching them those responsibilities. So, there was a great deal of thinking associated with this heading, until we sat down to dinner! Having several young adults around a table is a constant source of inspiration as you listen to their accounts of revulsion and grandeur mixed together.

So, it was with the tales of the manufacture of Chocolate and Wine at the dinner table that I am able to accomplish my quest. I will not go into the gory details; or you would never eat chocolate or drink wine again, that is, if you don't already know the ghastly facts about bugs and snakes.

As I listened to the point where I was having trouble keeping my food down I thought about how life can be filled with unsavoury moments and great danger. These things are just part of life. No matter how careful we are we will always find ourselves facing these things and the consequences will often mean that we have to move through the process of grief. However, just like the Chocolate and Wine, we will be transformed into something that is precious.

"And we know that all things work together for good to them that love God, to them who are the called according to his purpose." (Romans 8:28).

4. Attention Please

Those who know me understand that I am not a great animal lover, but when the children were little we decided that they could have a cat, hoping that it might work. as a mouse catcher. So, our farm has always had a resident cat or two. As I was hanging out the washing one morning one of our cats decided that it liked me. It tried all sorts of things to get my attention. First, it played with my toes, then rubbed my legs, and had another go at my toes. Finally, as I walked back to the house it followed me, it wasn't until I shut the door firmly that it decided to do something else.

As it was trying to get my attention, I thought, this is just like Jesus. He came into our world, *"And no man hath ascended up to heaven, but he that came down from heaven, even the Son of man which is in heaven."* (John 3:13). Why did He do that? He did that to show us that He loves us. *"For God so loved the world that He gave His only begotten Son, that whosoever believeth in Him should not perish but have everlasting life."* (John 3:16). He wants us to respond to Him and He tries many ways to get our attention.

Just like my response to the cat, we can respond with love or we can firmly shut the door to Him. He doesn't force us to love Him. He is patient, working through the Holy Spirit to show us how we have sinned, how much He loves us and what He has done for us. *"If we confess our sins, he is faithful and just to forgive us our sins, and to cleanse us from all unrighteousness"* 1 John 1:9.

Will you respond or will you shut the door?

5. Bedside

As I looked at the papers strewn all over the bedside table one afternoon, a sigh escapes. The mess doesn't mean I am disorganised, but, just how easy it is to be buried by the work of life. I work sitting on my bed for two reasons. Firstly, my back does not like my office chair. Secondly, the internet signal is better here.

Some people will tell you that in order to have the correct mindset about your work you should dress and set up your workplace as if you are going to the office. Others will tell you that if you want to sleep well then, your bed should be exclusively for sleeping, not reading, not computer work or eating – just sleeping. This would mean that I break all these rules most of the time. I have to admit that there are some days where if you were to surprise me with a visit you might get the impression that I was bedridden.

This doesn't mean that I ignore all the other jobs that need to be done. They still get completed and there are days when I fear I will wear out the springs by getting up and down so many times. I get to enjoy the view through the window while I write and work at those more unsavoury jobs on my agenda.

I am glad that God allows me to work in this way and blesses what I do, however small my part is. *"For the LORD your God has blessed you in everything you have done. He has watched your every step through this great wilderness. During these forty years, the LORD your God has been with you, and you have lacked nothing."* Deuteronomy 2:7 even if nobody else understands or approves I'm pretty sure He does.

6. Being Content

Recently we had a visit from one of our children, who surveyed a patch of garden that had been tidied up; to let a grapevine get some much-needed sun. What did you do that for? It looks bare! This was in contrast to numerous previous discussions about these particular plants needing to be removed because they looked ugly. As you can imagine my response was "It wouldn't matter what we did you wouldn't be happy" and their answer was yeah, you're right! Some people just never seem to be content.

In Hebrews 13:1-6 Paul instructs us to be content in whatever situation we find ourselves in. By asking us to not forget to entertain strangers, he is telling us that we need to be content to show hospitality to them. That's not hard I hear you say, we know when we are having visitors and we can be prepared for them. Really? What about those unexpected callers, or those who want to visit when we are busy and have a lot to do, are we then content to sit, talk and listen to visitors then, particularly those in need of a long-suffering listening ear. God tells us that we might be entertaining angels unawares, even if they do seem like the devil sometimes.

Secondly, we are told to be content with what we have and remember that not everyone has the blessings that we do. Those people who are struggling, physically, emotionally, or spiritually are our brothers and sisters, even if they are not brothers and sisters in Christ, we are still connected in our common humanity. These days with the fast transmission of information we now are informed about so many people who are in need. It can be overwhelming and very easy to dismiss bad news in order to protect our own sense of wellbeing. Do we spend some part of our day in prayer for them, or do we dismiss their plight as a result of their lack of good judgement and consider it a deserved consequence?

Next, we should be content with our relationships. No relationship is perfect, but we must remember that God has a plan for our lives and that plan includes our partners regardless of our faults and theirs. Matthew Henry reminds us that we have nothing to be discontent with. We are so blessed by the faithfulness of God who will supply all our needs. He will never leave us and that is why we have nothing to worry about, we do not need to fear hunger, homelessness, or anything that this world can dish out, as God will always be with us.

Paul reinforces this in Philippians 4:12 "I know what it is to be in need, and I know what it is to have plenty. I have learned the secret of being content in any and every situation, whether well fed or hungry, whether living in plenty or in want." This business of being content is something that we need to teach ourselves, it's a choice that we have to make each time we are faced with something that we are tempted to feel discontented about. So next time we feel a little hint of dissatisfaction let us remember that the choice to be content is ours, as hard as it is, it's what God wants us to learn.

As we learn to be satisfied with what we have, we will be able to increasingly say more boldly *"The Lord is my helper and I will not fear what man shall do unto me."* Hebrews 13:6.

7. Borrowed

I was borrowed, one day, to look after my great-grandson. His mother had an appointment to keep and needed someone to babysit him. As I thought about what I could write under this heading I realised that we borrow a lot of things and if we are to borrow, someone has to lend. It's not the opposite of borrow but goes hand in hand.

We often have to borrow something because we have forgotten to be prepared. Ever gone somewhere without a coat or jumper (sweater) and the weather has turned cold. Usually, someone is willing to lend you something to help keep you warm.

The thing about something being borrowed is that you only have possession of it for a short period of time.

It is often said that our children are lent to us, not given. We bring home our newborn babies and after about the first six weeks we think that this parenting job is going to go on forever and a day. Then one day we watch our children walk out the door and realise that our time with them is over. We ask ourselves wasn't it just yesterday that we brought our baby home? They have their own lives, our role as parents has shifted into a different gear in this thing called life. When you think about it, we realise that life is actually borrowed time. We are here for such a short while, and then we have to go back to our creator.

"Whereas ye know not what shall be on the morrow. For what is your life? It is even a vapour, that appeareth for a little time, and then vanisheth away."
James 4:14.

When we borrow something, it is our responsibility to look after it and return it to the owner in a very good condition. Do we?

8. Christmas Night

A few years ago, I was leaving the house at midnight. As I had to do this nearly every night, I got into the habit of checking the sky before getting into my car. On this particular night, it was a perfect black velvet with diamond stars. Yes, just like it would be described in a storybook.

As I looked up, I thought that it was a perfect Christmas night sky. As I thought about it later, I had to ask myself why we consider that sort of sky to be a Christmassy one. There is no weather report in the Bible about the night Jesus was born. So why do we come up with this assumption? The conclusion I came to was that it was these sorts of nights, that you don't expect anything dramatic to happen and if it did it would be quite a shock.

On another night, on a walk that started at dusk, I watched as the night sky darkened to what would eventually end up being another velvet and diamond sky. However, over the distant mountains, there was an electrical storm brewing with flashes of lightning. Even though I knew that the storm far away from our place and wasn't going to affect us, I must admit to flinching every time there was a flash. Now if I flinched when I knew what was happening, I can only imagine how those shepherds felt on that first Christmas night. *"And there were in the same country shepherds abiding in the field, keeping watch over their flock by night. And, lo, the angel of the Lord came upon them, and the glory of the Lord shone round about them: and they were sore afraid."*
Luke 2:8-9.

It does not surprise me that they were afraid. They had no idea what was happening. How the angel was able to relieve their fears, I have no idea. Yet they seemed to become calm and had the presence of mind to make the decision to go and see this babe that God had told them about. "When the angels had left them and gone into heaven, the shepherds said to one another, "Let's go to Bethlehem and see this thing that has happened, which the Lord has told us about." Luke 2:15

Their courage was rewarded, they got to see Jesus and share with Mary and Joseph the joy that comes with the birth of a baby, in this case, a very special baby. *"So, they hurried off and found Mary and Joseph, and the baby, who was lying in the manger."* Luke 2:16.

I'm sure they were very pleased that they managed to get past their fear and were able to receive the blessing of being the first to see the special gift that God had for the whole world.

1. Closed Door

How many times have you come up against a closed door? You know about the times I'm talking about. When circumstances block your entry into some area of endeavour you can either push harder, relax, and wait or walk away. Closed doors are, however, not the same as locked doors. Many women throughout history have had to push into the areas of endeavour that they had previously been considered locked out of.

In the past, many jobs were considered to be inappropriate for women to carry out. Personally, I take my hat off to any woman who worked under the social and physical conditions that existed. I am so very grateful to the women who have worked so hard to improve conditions for us. These women have often had to push very hard against some of those doors that appeared to be closed. Even today many women have to continue to march forward into career areas that are still considered more suitable to the male population.

Of course, it's not only women who have had to push hard to ensure that progress happens in our world. There are the reformers of the Victoria era, such as Captain Cook who sailed around the world to find Australia. There was also William Wilberforce who fought for years to abolish slavery in the 18th century. Closer to home there is the long list of explorers who pushed through the Australian bush and deserts to find out more about our wide amazing country.

Modern door pushers are those who are working on the exploration of outer space, modern technology and medical research but, I fear that we are going to have to revisit those doors that have seemed to have slammed closed again, such as human rights, education and social conditions for people living in less fortunate circumstances.

10. Clouds

Today I woke early and checked the sky. I wanted to know what the weather might be like on this particular day and one way of trying to work that out was to see what sort of clouds were out there in the sky. I had a load of washing to do and I wanted to see if it would get dry. There was a reasonable thick layer of clouds so, I would need most of the day to achieve that. After breakfast I took the load of washing to the clothes hoist and again checked the sky, it was clear blue and there was a nice light breeze stirring the leaves on nearby trees.

The washing dried and as I looked at the sky again later that evening, I could see through the window that a light covering of clouds had returned.

What was the message for me on this wonderful successful washing day? God seemed to be reminding me that clouds in life will come and go; they will never be a permanent feature in my life. I remembered my mother telling me when I was younger that the most common phrase in the Bible was "And it came to pass". As a youngster, I had wondered what that quaint phrase really meant. I realised that it meant what it said, that both good and bad things will come and go. Nothing in this world will last forever.

"While we look not at the things which are seen, but at the things which are not seen: for the things which are seen are temporal; but the things which are not seen are eternal." 2 Corinthians 4:18.

Let us all take comfort that at least the word of God will last forever.

11. Colour

The sun is rising across the valley and slowly I get to see the colours of my world again. They have been there all night but hidden under the blanket of darkness and sleep.

So, what happens each morning when I watch the sun rise and it lightens my world. It reminds me that there are good things in my life. They may just have been hidden under a blanket of pain, illness, or depression but the truth is they are still there. I just cannot see them during these times.

Some of us may not like the colours we see when the sun rises. I'm thinking of our poor drought-affected farmers who only see brown dirt and pale blue skies when they look around them. They need the skies to turn grey. So that rain will fall and turn brown mud into green grass. I pray that they too will remember that someday it will happen.

In Psalm 30:5 we read: *"For his anger edureth but a moment; in his favour is life; weeping may endure for a night, but joy cometh in the morning."*

Yes, it is hard to hang on to these truths when we are having a bad day, week, or year. The truth is, however, the truth and a bad day doesn't change that. It's like gravity, you can believe all you like that it doesn't exist but when you jump off a cliff, gravity works. It takes you to the bottom, and it takes you there fast.

When we are in the middle of bad days, which seem to go on forever, I pray that we will always remember that God declares that the sun has to rise in the morning and we can claim the promise from Psalm 126:5 *"They that sow in tears shall reap in joy."*

12. Dark

We all have to face those dark days. Those days will vary, from ones where everything seems to go wrong to days when bad news sends your world into a complete spin.

"A Psalm of David. The LORD is my shepherd; I shall not want. He maketh me to lie down in green pastures: he leadeth me beside the still waters. He restoreth my soul: he leadeth me in the paths of righteousness for his name's sake. Yea, though I walk through the valley of the shadow of death, I will fear no evil: for thou art with me; thy rod and thy staff they comfort me. Thou preparest a table before me in the presence of mine enemies: thou anointest my head with oil; my cup runneth over. Surely goodness and mercy shall follow me all the days of my life: and I will dwell in the house of the LORD for ever." Psalm 23.

As we enter the valleys of life, we have no idea how dark, deep, and long they will be but the best we can do is hold the hand of our Lord and walk forward in faith knowing that He will be with us all the way.

"Have not I commanded thee? Be strong and of a good courage; be not afraid, neither be thou dismayed: for the LORD thy God is with thee whithersoever thou goest." Joshua 1:9.

The other thing we have to keep in mind, is that no matter how dark long and deep the valley is, there will be an end to it and we will one day stand on high ground again.

13. Depth of Field

When I think about this I generally think about the depth of soil in my husband's paddocks or field. If it's not that it's wondering how far down the moisture levels are.

How far down the water has managed to soak in, is important to farmers? How deep the good soil is, is also very important. Both these things are pretty much out of our control. The good topsoil can be removed from the higher places by wind and rain and deposited on the lower valleys by the same elements.

Yes, we can help protect the paddocks by leaving or planting trees, but we cannot undo the work already done in a hurry. It takes time, years in fact.

The same thing happens with people. It takes years for them to grow in maturity. We would not expect a one-week-old baby to talk let alone have knowledge that we have accumulated over our lifetime.

When people become Christians, we need to be patient, understanding and tolerant because they are still young in spirit, if not years. They need time to grow, to learn and to understand. Just as we cannot put old heads on young shoulders in the normal world, so we can't put old spiritual heads on young spiritual shoulders.

How much depth and maturity they will develop is also pretty much out of our hands because it is only God who waters and tends the fields of our spiritual lives. "So then neither is he that planteth anything, neither he that watereth; but God that giveth the increase." (1 Corinthians 3:7).

14. Details

I was reading a story recently; it was one of those where they tell two connected stories dovetailed together. Suddenly I stopped and reread the line I had just finished. All I thought was that they have put the wrong character in here.

What aggravated me the most was how irritated I felt that they hadn't got the details right. It was a minor slip up and it didn't take away from the story. I find it very easy to do this in other areas of my life as well.

We get so caught up in details and issues that we miss the context of life.

I'm not saying that people shouldn't do a job properly, they should. Compassion is a good thing when mistakes are made and we need to remember that no one is perfect.

Psalm 86:15 says: *"But thou, O Lord, art a God full of compassion, and gracious, longsuffering, and plenteous in mercy and truth."* And we are instructed in Ephesians 5:1-2 to *"Be ye therefore followers of God, as dear children; and walk in love, as Christ also hath loved us, and hath given himself for us an offering and a sacrifice to God for a sweet smelling savour."*

Yes, I know I often fail at this and sadly the older I get the less success I seem to have at this task. Either way, I know that God loves me and will not give up on me even though I am tempted to give up on myself.

15. Dinner

There is something very satisfying about a good meal. It makes you feel comfortably filled. Sometimes it can bring on a sleepiness that can take over making afternoon laziness a tempting option particularly after a mid-day dinner.

Cooking a good meal is hard work and then there is cleaning up to be done afterwards. If you are the cook, putting all that hard work into a meal, means it can be upsetting when it isn't eaten or is just toyed with. In some countries, I understand that if you add anything, such as salt, pepper, or sauce you are insulting the cook. I also understand that in other countries it is appropriate to make what we consider rude noises after a meal in order to show appreciation for the meal. The thing is, any meal is something that a lot of love and effort has been given in order to feed us and it is easy to make them feel unappreciated or insult those wonderful people.

Yet we can do the same to God, we can ignore the love and care that He shows us on a daily basis. Sometimes we are even unaware of what we are doing. *"Consider the ravens: for they neither sow nor reap; which neither have storehouse nor barn; and God feedeth them: how much more are ye better than the fowls?"*
Luke 12:24.

Some people reject everything that Jesus has done for them. *"He that rejecteth me, and receiveth not my words, hath one that judgeth him: the word that I have spoken, the same shall judge him in the last day."* John 12:48. God cares for us in many ways and often in ways that we may never know about. So, at the end of each day let us thank Him anyway.

16. Drink

When I think about the word Drink, I can tell you that my favourite drink is tea. In fact, I could very well be addicted to it. I do occasionally prove this not to be the case as I have been known to go a whole day with only one or two cups even if it is rarely. The only other drink that my health issues allow me to indulge in is Soda Water.

When we think about drinking, we think about refreshment, relaxing after a long day at work or just having fun with friends and family. This is often with some variety of alcoholic beverages. Of course, there are those that abuse the whole concept. We see reports on the news most weekends telling sad stories of bad behaviour, fights, car accidents and lives ruined because of the abuse of such substances.

I decided early on in life to remain a "teetotaller" based on the knowledge that my great grandfather was, for part of his life, an alcoholic. Once he gave control of his life to Jesus, he was able to give up the drink and live a life that was productive in business and service of his God and church.

In his first letter to Timothy, Paul instructs him to stop drinking water and take a little wine for his stomach. (1 Timothy 5:23). It appears that there was a problem with the quality of the water that was available and that the wine was to be used in order to help the ailment.

Despite the warnings from various people that tea is not good for me, I will for the moment keep drinking it. I'm sure one day they will find that it has some benefit for me.

17. Eight O'clock

What could be special about 8 O'clock? After all, it's only another hour that has ticked by once already. It does occur to me that 8 O'clock in the evening is not really 8 O'clock. If we talk about time in terms of twenty-four hours – 8 o'clock is twenty hours into the day.

This got me thinking about what words we use that have two meanings. The first one that came to mind is the word "fear". We are told in Joshua 1:9 *"This is my command--be strong and courageous! Do not be afraid or discouraged. For the LORD your God is with you wherever you go."* And yet in Proverbs 9:10, we are told *"Fear of the LORD is the foundation of wisdom. Knowledge of the Holy One results in good judgment."*

In the first verse, we are told not to be scared of what is happening around us. Some people have been told to be afraid of a judgemental God. If we do something wrong, He will strike us down lighting but this is not the sort of God we have. We have a loving God, a God who is just and fair. While we are here on earth, He will reach out to us and forgive us when we ask Him. *"And I will forgive their wickedness, and I will never again remember their sins."* Hebrews 8:12.

The other verse that tells us that the fear of the Lord is the beginning of wisdom refers to being so amazed at what God can do, that we just stand there and watch His wonderful plan unfold.

This is of course not a literal thing, otherwise we would get nothing done, but like me I am sure that sometimes you just cannot help but be staggered by what our God does.

18. Energy

It had been one of those days that most of us have every now and then where at every turn something goes wrong. I was spending a lot of time in tears or on the phone trying to find out what was happening and not making much progress on whatever front I was working on. Fortunately, the sun was out and there was a stiff breeze blowing. This meant that I could use the energy from the sun to freshen up my pillows and the wind was able to dry my washing. The washing machine didn't spin the clothes out properly and it was hung out very wet. There was still the question of how I was to be energised.

The night before I had been reading about some of the great preachers in our history and discovered that many of them had suffered from depression just like me. Depression sucks the life out of you, and I was finding that this was certainly the case on this occasion. I remembered that David had also suffered in a similar way. So many of the Psalms start out with David feeling vulnerable and lonely but end with him praising the God and Lord of his life.

I am beginning to understand that depression isn't a sin, it's an emotional illness! Like all emotions, they can cause us to sin if we let them control us. Ephesians 4:26 tells us *"Be ye angry, and sin not: let not the sun go down upon your wrath:"* but these words can apply to any emotion, happiness, joy, depression, and grief. What I had to realise was that I cannot solve a problem by looking at it. Hebrews 12:2a holds the answer *"Looking unto Jesus the author and finisher of our faith;"* and He gives me energy.

19. Faceless Self-portrait

Nothing frustrates us more than being controlled or directed by what society has named 'those faceless men'. They are the people who appear to make decisions without actually having any first-hand or practical experience of a given situation.

I'm pretty sure there are days when people don't want to see my face, particularly if I am tired, angry, or sad. As a mother, there are very few if any, days when I can hide away from my family and the world. As humans we are very interested in faces, they help us to read people and understand how they feel. When people talk to us, we can read in their faces if they are serious or if they are trying to tease us.

Of course, humans have always been interested in faces. Even Moses wanted to see the face of God. He wasn't allowed to, because it would have killed him. *"And he said, I beseech thee, shew me thy glory. And he said, I will make all my goodness pass before thee, and I will proclaim the name of the LORD before thee; and will be gracious to whom I will be gracious, and will shew mercy on whom I will shew mercy."* Exodus 33:18-20.

While I am quite happy not to see the face of God here on earth, I know that one day I will see Him face to face and that will be a very awesome experience indeed.

20. Fake

As I looked around the room, I noticed some flowers sitting on top of the bookshelf. They looked beautiful, just like the real ones. Yes, they would last longer than real ones and they didn't have that wonderful perfume that real ones had, because they were FAKE.

I prefer real ones because there is always a perfume even if the perfume is not nice. Some flowers smell awful but there are many more that smell lovely and I love to enjoy their presence in my house.

Some perfumes invoke good memories, others bad memories. Some people do the same. Some people come across as being real and others seem to have life so good that you have to wonder if they are lying and therefore fake.

The Bible also tells us that we can be fake Christians, "And the Lord said: *"Because this people draw near with their mouth and honour me with their lips, while their hearts are far from me, and their fear of me is a commandment taught by men,"* Isaiah 29:13

So, my prayer today is that I will always be real, not fake when it comes to not only my worship of my Lord but also the way I live my life each and every day.

21. Favourite

My favourite pastime at present is writing short stories. I feel that I am not very good at it and I am always amazed when people tell me that I am talented. When I was at school, I had trouble with reading, spelling, and arithmetic.

My break came when I reached thirty-something, it was discovered that I had an eye co-ordination problem. It turned out that my eyes were not working together in the way that they should have been. To explain it further; if you gave me the number 12, my left eye would see the one and my right eye would see the two. My brain then had to work out if the number was 12 or 21. In the meantime, the class had moved on. Spelling presented similar issues.

So, my desire to write seemed like an impossible dream. Until God allowed someone to invent the computer and more importantly 'spell checker'. I still use that facility a lot. Without this technology, I would never be able to write a short story, let alone three hundred and fifty-five of them. There are still days when my lack of skills really gets me down and I feel as if I am truly out of my depth.

On these occasions, I have to remind myself that God has helped me to do this. What His reasons are I have no idea but I will keep going for the moment and I praise Him each time someone is encouraged by something that I present.

There are two verses that keep coming to mind during those bad moments that I have and they are: *"I can do all things through Christ which strengtheneth me."* Philippians 4:13 and *"For my thoughts are not your thoughts, neither are your ways my ways, saith the LORD."* Isaiah 55:8

22. Fear

I had run out of sticky tape. I was in a hurry. I couldn't remember where the new rolls were, so I start searching, one drawer at a time. I pulled open one particular drawer, looked down and there sitting on top of my ink packs was a spider. Now, I'm not really afraid of these creatures, unlike one of my daughters, but I pulled back quickly enough.

A quick surface look revealed that the said "sticky tape" wasn't to be found without things being moved around. I didn't poke around and do a thorough search. Fortunately for me as I turned around a new roll almost jumped up and bit me. Why I hadn't seen it lying there before is probably because I was in such a hurry.

At the time of writing I was checking out some things on Facebook and from some of the posts I could see what a powerful force fear was. You can see it as the motivation behind what people do and say. It is also a force that will prevent people from doing what they may, should or would like to do.

Psalm 118:6 says: *"The LORD is on my side; I will not fear: what can man do unto me?"* Yes, they can do a lot to us, we see the evidence of that every night on the news and it could cause some of us to freak out. There have definitely been times when I have been frozen with fear myself and thankfully God has sent someone along to remind me of the truth.

"And fear not them which kill the body, but are not able to kill the soul: but rather fear him which is able to destroy both soul and body in hell." Matthew 10:28

23. Flash or Dash

As a teenager and learner driver, one of my sons purchased his first car. It had a large spoiler and body kit, being bright green, it looked every bit as good as any race car. However, when you drove it, you soon realised that it had nowhere near the power of my plain looking car of the same make. Now as a mother I had no problem with this because it meant that as a learner driver (and we learn for many years after we get our licences) this was a good car for my son. There was not enough power in it, for him to get into some situations that he might not be able to get out of. Yes, he could still make a fatal mistake or get hurt or killed, as a consequence of other's actions but the lack of power meant there were some limits.

So, while this car had a lot of flash, there was not a lot of dash in it. I realised that the same could be said about some people. Some people can look like they have it all together but put them under some pressure and they fall apart, lose their temper, or just plain don't cope.

The Bible tells us not to look at the exterior but get to know people properly. In 1 Samuel 16:7b when Samuel goes looking for a new king for Israel, and God tells him *"... for the Lord seeth not as man seeth for man looketh on the outward appearance but the Lord looketh on the heart."*

James talks about this issue in James 2:1-13. The title in my Bible says: 'Faith Removes Discrimination', proving that with the help of the Holy Spirit we can see what is flash or real dash.

24. Floral

I'm old enough to have had to attend Home Economic classes at school. For those that don't understand what I am talking about, they were classes to teach girls how to cook, sew, wash up and carry out home duties. One of the units each year was "Floral Art". I didn't pass with great marks. It was considered back then an essential skill as a homemaker. I just realised we weren't taught gardening skills in these classes, however, were the flowers to appear by magic or was it considered the man's job to produce the flowers. I must confess to some memory loss on that front.

Floral Art from my poor memory, had elements of proportion, balance, form and sometimes a theme. Some arrangements go as far as to tell a story. Yes, I did think about this too but haven't had the courage to go there yet. Each floral arrangement would be different, and you kept it fresh by sticking it in the fridge each night. Our fridge would never have the room!

Some people are able to live their lives according to these rules as well applying, proportion, balance and form, to how much time they give to work, children, families and church. Some of us though are a lot like me when it comes to floral art. I pick some flowers; pull off the unnecessary leaves, find a vase, fill it with water and plonk the flowers in. They still look great, they smell wonderful, particularly if I have cut roses or jonquils and they brighten up the whole room.

I just get things done when I can, dropping everything to assist other members of the family and so on, but hopefully I can brighten up someone's life and made them feel a little better.

25. Food

Oh, what a subject for me to write about. My family has so many issues that I have been known to say that food is pretty much a "four-letter word" for me. I posted this once and someone said, "but it is a four-letter word" my response was "each time I think about food I want to swear". Looking forward to my old age I just shudder about what food might be available if I am to be confined to an institution.

I need to remember that I can at least still eat. Many others cannot. I am blessed simply because God selected Australia as the place for me to live. He also blessed me with the time in history that He selected for me. Had I been born in previous centuries I would have been very ill or died at a very early age. So, while the whole issue of food annoys me quite a bit, I have to remember on a daily basis that I am very blessed.

Of course, the other thing that I need to remember is that while I need food to survive. It can be overindulged in. That will, and has, created other problems to be dealt with. Along with this, there is one other thing that I need to remember. In Deuteronomy 8:3 we read *"And he humbled thee, and suffered thee to hunger, and fed thee with manna, which thou knewest not, neither did thy fathers know; that he might make thee know that man doth not live by bread only, but by every word that proceedeth out of the mouth of the LORD doth man live."* So, while food can be a trial, the Lord knows exactly what I need and can use it to teach me lessons as well.

26.

Once again, I have forgotten that the muffins were in the oven. As I thought about why we forget things I realised that it is often because something else becomes more important. In this particular case, Facebook got in the road. On other occasions, it's been the needs of children, grandchildren, or paperwork.

Why, you ask, would you walk away from a job when you know it has to be completed? You see when people are busy; they have trouble waiting for things to happen. After all, another job shouldn't take more than ten minutes and you should be back in plenty of time to finish off the job you started with. The problem is, of course, that what starts out to be a ten-minute job often ends up being a twenty or thirty minute one.

Of course, this can happen on a spiritual level as well. How many times have you asked someone about their spiritual health and they have replied along the lines of, "I'm too busy to think about it just now" or "I deal with that when I have more time"? I know, I have come across some people who have said similar things to me.

Sometimes, I myself have slipped into a situation where I have been too busy to give God and His plan for my life much thought. It doesn't mean that I have forgotten Him but He has been pushed into the back of my mind for a short time.

So many times throughout scripture we are instructed to: "……..*Thou shalt love the Lord thy God with all thy heart, and with all thy soul, and with all thy strength, and with all thy mind; and thy neighbour as thyself.*" Luke 10:27, see also Matthew 22:37, Mark 12:30-31, Deuteronomy 6:5.

27. Four O'clock

When the clock strikes four it's a signal that it is now time to carry out some jobs. There are cats, dogs, and chooks to be fed. In the winter, wood needs to be collected and if there is washing on the line, it has to be brought in. There is also an evening meal to be cooked.

There will always be days when no one feels like getting up and doing all these duties. But duty calls to all of us at some time. As I sit in front of my heater on a very cold autumn day, my enthusiasm for going outside is really lacking. Oh, how I would love to pass the buck.

Yet as I close the week, thinking about my grandfather, Robert Archibald Deans, and all those men who went off to war because they would not shirk their duty; I have to feel a little shame. Many of those men, who were called up for service, didn't want to fight, they hated killing, they saw it as evil and still, they did their duty! Yes, they marched into battle, determined to make sure that the country that they called home would be a safe place for their loved ones. It was to be the war that would end all wars. I don't know if they really believed that, I doubt it, but then maybe I'm just a little too cynical because I know that it didn't deliver on that promise.

There is one other person who did not draw back from his duty and that was Jesus. He went to the cross because He loved us, and His promises to forgive us when we come to Him and He always delivers on His promises.

28. Free

One of the most difficult jobs my husband has to do as a result of the drought is to pull sheep free from the mud when they get stuck in the dam. Some people just cannot understand why they would be silly enough to get stuck in dams particularly when there is water available at a water trough in the same paddock.

These sheep, however, are not really that different to people, are they? Some people when they find themselves in desperate circumstances move headlong into the situation that had consequences they had not anticipated. They find themselves in a situation that they are unable to get out of without the assistance of someone bigger, stronger, more powerful, and sometimes smarter.

Those of us standing on the sidelines of these peoples' lives sometimes shake our heads and wonder how they managed to get into such a mess. We can judge and debate about why they didn't take up other options that were available. We can declare that we wouldn't get into the same mess and maybe we wouldn't but that is us not them. We cannot know what we would do if we were that person, with their history, makeup, and emotional state.

There is someone however who does know them inside out because He has made them, watched them, cried with them, and cared for them. He is someone, who is bigger, stronger more powerful and smarter and He can help them.

Psalm 40:1-2 *"I waited patiently for the Lord and he inclined unto me and heard my cry. He brought me up also out of an horrible pit, out of the miry clay and set my foot upon a rock and established my goings."* If we call on God to help, He will be there, all we have to do, is ask.

29. From Where I Stand

At this point in my life, from where I stand, my life looks a little foggy. I can't see my future and the rest of my road seems covered in a fog of uncertainty. There are so many things that I would like to do and so many things that may or may not happen. When I manage to do some of the things that I would like to do. This body of mine complains quite a bit these days. I find myself so tired afterwards that I wonder if I will ever have enough energy to do anything I want to. I was given a gift once that says "Dreams don't work unless you do." I don't feel particularly old until I start working hard and then my body starts to tell me a different story.

I am certain that I am not the only person that is standing where I stand. In order to move forward, I must walk in faith. I must hold the hand of my Lord and keep going one step at a time. *"Now faith is confidence in what we hope for and assurance about what we do not see."* Hebrews 11:1 so *"For we walk by faith, not by sight."* 1 Corinthians 5:7

One thing I am certain of and can clearly see in my mind's eye is that one day I will be standing in front of the throne of God *"And as it is appointed unto men once to die, but after this the judgment:"* Hebrews 9:27. With that look of love He will say welcome my child you worked hard for me and I will bow my head in shame and say 'but Lord you know my heart'. I wait in faith for His response.

30. Frozen Water

Water does things differently to other liquids when it freezes. It expands rather than shrinks. In this process of freezing its power can break anything that may try to confine it, such as a bottle, even a rock. As hail, depending on the size of those hailstones, the damage can be quite devastating when it really smashes things. If it freezes while dripping it creates the most beautiful icicles. When snow covers a community in a blanket of white, we see beauty that can stagger the imagination.

Like ice, we can also do things differently through the power of God. We can be beautiful, sparkling as we endeavour to live more and more like Jesus each day. Showing others how much He cares for the people that He created. Throughout history, many Christians have managed to break quite a few of the social issues that have confined people in difficult circumstances. I am thinking of William Wilberforce and his work to abolish slavery and Caroline Chisholm and her work amongst the convict women during the early days of Australia's European settlement. These people worked hard and consistently for many years were able to smash what were great social injustices.

No matter what God calls us to do, in order to make this world a better place to live we can be reassured that He will give us all that we need to accomplish it *"I can do all things through Christ who strengthens me."* Philippians 4:13.

At the very least if we live our lives through God's spirit, we will make our world a much nicer place and give some people some extra beauty.

31. Fruit to Sauce

My husband found a couple of plum trees on another property that we own. He picked a small quantity and brought them home. His plan was to feed them to the chooks, but I decided to have a go at making plum sauce. I have never been very good at this sort of cooking, but I was willing to give it a go. If the final product was no good, then the chooks could still eat it even if it was in a different form.

So, the plums went into the pot along with the sugar, vinegar, ginger, salt, and peppers. I sat it on the stove and left it to cook while I managed to carry out other duties. A couple of hours later I came back and started to remove the seeds which had been left in and continued to wonder if this was going to be any good to eat.

As I was doing this, I reflected on how this could be related to our lives. Is it a wonder to anyone else that we start off being just plain people and then as we grow up, we have various experiences that could be described as salt, sugar, vinegar, spice, or heat from the stove? These experiences help change us as people; our attitude to them will mould us into the sorts of adults that we grow up to be. How is it that some people become mature, capable, and useful while others just don't seem to cope, they can't even hold down a job or manage with day to day activities? These are the mysteries of life.

God does not want us to break through the experiences of life, He wants us to grow strong and powerful. Check out Revelation 3:19, Hebrews 12:6 and Proverbs 3:12.

32. Get Moving

I had developed another health issue and I wasn't happy. I had just finished recovering from the last one and I wanted to stay well and healthy. Something I suppose that is not really possible at my age. However, this particular morning I was so busy moaning about the issue that I nearly forgot to take the medicine that is to help fix the problem.

God tapped me on the shoulder. There is no point moaning about an issue if you don't do something about it. There are, of course, times when you are unable to do anything, but when the solution is right there it's time to get up and get moving. Not only did I take my medicine but I even managed to get outside and started working on my garden which needs a lot of problems fixed.

There is a lot of talk around the world at present in view of what has happened in the Middle East, yet there doesn't seem to be a lot of action. What can we do to help and fix this problem? Not a lot physically, but we can pray, pray, and pray some more.

The real solution to these problems is in the revival of people from the inside, not external forces.

"For this very reason, make every effort to supplement your faith with virtue, and virtue with knowledge, and knowledge with self-control, and self-control with steadfastness, and steadfastness with godliness, and godliness with brotherly affection, and brotherly affection with love. For if these qualities are yours and are increasing, they keep you from being ineffective or unfruitful in the knowledge of our Lord Jesus Christ." 2 Peter 1:5-8.

Yes, we will have to really pray about what it is that God wants us to do and there are voices out there that will tell us that we are not making a difference but God sees everything that we do, no matter how small it is.

33. God Sees You

I was hanging a picture in the spare room recently. After I had picked the spot on the wall, I just happened to look down and found a memento from a wedding, shredded to pieces. It had obviously been hidden there, out of the way, in order to conceal its destruction. I could guess as to who was responsible, but I could be wrong and it's not that the item was valuable. The first verse that came to mind was *"But if ye will not do so, behold, ye have sinned against the LORD: and be sure your sin will find you out."* Numbers 32:23.

It did, however, get me thinking about why we hide things away in cupboards. Is it really to make the place look tidy? We are not always trying to cover up something of course, but I have to wonder if we aren't trying to hide things from our family members and friends. I know that sometimes things are put away in order to protect our privacy.

I thought about my parents and their lives when they were small children. I remember, my mum telling me that they didn't have cupboards to put things away in. In one house, they only had wooden boxes stacked on top of each other to store things in. Maybe it's just a case of us having too much stuff to look after.

It's not just things that we try to hide either, often its things we don't like about our looks or personalities, that we try to cover up. I could tell when one of my children was stressed because he would talk in his sleep; another would get overactive when he was nervous. I have often coloured my hair in order to make myself look a little less drained to the world.

Whatever it is that we are trying to hide we need to remember that no matter where we are or what we are doing, God sees all of it. *"Neither is there any creature that is not manifest in his sight: but all things are naked and opened unto the eyes of him with whom we have to do."* Hebrews 4:13.

34. God Sings — Psalm 95:1-7

On a recent trip to visit family, we spent a couple of nights close to the ocean. As I laid down waiting for sleep to take over, I listened to the noises around me. Each new place has different sounds. One particular noise dominated the night and it took me a while to register that the sound was actually the waves crashing on the beach. Once I realised what it was, I listened with a different attitude and decided that it was God's lullaby to help me get to sleep.

Of course, on the morning before we left for home, we went for a walk along the beach, you cannot be that close to the beach and not do that, no matter how much you might not be a fan of sand and saltwater. On this particular stretch of beach, there was a reef of rocks which I realised helped make the lullaby that I had been listening to during the nights there! What I saw was the power of God at work. I saw big rocks that had been turned into small smooth pebbles and the sea that stretched as far as the eye could see. Only a God as amazing as the God of creation could do such a miraculous thing.

And just think, He did so by saying eleven words: *"Then God said, "Let the waters beneath the sky flow together into one place, so dry ground may appear."* And that is what happened. Genesis 1:9.

Do you hear God singing when you look at His wonderful creation around you?

35. Gone Fishing

I was listening to a discussion on fishing. It revolved around the issues of when, where and how to pick the best place to go fishing. There was also a comment made that if all these things were not at their optimal then it was a waste of time to fish. I felt my hackles rising. I'm no fisherman/person (for those that want me to be politically correct) but I know from what others have to say it seems that landing fish is not the only benefit of going fishing. If for instance, you go fishing in what is considered the wrong place, then maybe you will be surprised with an unexpected catch. If you go at the wrong time you could still be flabbergasted by that elusive fish latching on to the hook. If you don't catch a thing, other than a cold, you have had the opportunity to relax, spend time with God, admire His handiwork and take time out to worship Him. Yes, right there on the riverbank you can worship Him.

The illustration was used in relation to being "fishers of men". That in order to catch men we must look for them in all the right places, making sure that all the conditions are right, or we are wasting our time. There is so much noise about wasting time, but the truth is that nothing is a waste of time. Yet, even as we acknowledge that God is in control we still have this problem of wanting to take over to "do" rather than let go and let God.

My first thoughts were of the disciples who were fishing all night in Luke 5; was it a waste of time for them to fish, and catch nothing? No! Through that experience, they were able to see the Glory of God, and Jesus used that to bring them to a point where they would be willing to follow Him.

Even when we think we are wasting time; God is still working in us. He has proved that to me over and over again!

I also recall a conversation with a work colleague who commented that maybe the younger generation had a better handle on life. They seemed better able to let go of the things that are not done in the time allotted to them. They relax in the knowledge that at some point they will get things done or if not, it won't matter. The point was, that our generation seems to be bent on wringing everything that they have out of life by working, stressing about what should be done and paying for it with their health.

This also seems to be catching on in church circles as well. We must work, be in the right place at the right time, and practice all the right things before we talk about God. My mother used to tell us that we needed to worry about what we needed to do before we worry about what other people should be doing. This also seems to be very good advice to all people. If we are doing what God wants us to do, we don't need to worry about what others are doing or what God is or isn't doing.

The truth is God doesn't need us to expand His kingdom. He doesn't need us to be here at all. He wants to involve us. He wants us to be available for Him to work through, but we must not get ahead of ourselves, EVER. We must always only be available and depend on Him to help and to grow in the fruits of the Spirit, as listed in Galatians 5:22-23, *"But the fruit of the Spirit is love, joy, peace, patience, kindness, goodness, faithfulness, gentleness and self-control."* Then He will work the most amazing miracles we will ever see. They may not be what we expect but they will be there if we only look.

36. Grow

We have a doorjamb which has been designated to recording the height of our children and grandchildren. It was something we didn't have when we were kids because we didn't own the houses that we lived in. I don't remember even having such a growth chart in the other two houses that we own either. I guess I felt deep down that we were only passing through these two places. Once we moved to the farm, I declared that my next move would happen in my "pine box". It had been such an undertaking that I really didn't and still don't want to do that again.

Let's go back to the growth chart. It surprises me that the children still measure themselves against the marks that are there even though they are adults now. You have to smile as parents compare their children to themselves and their Aunts and Uncles.

Growing taller is only one sign that we are growing. We have to grow inside as well. I often feel sad for those parents that do not experience this, for whatever reason, in their children. Yes, we all have days when we are frustrated with their behaviour but in the end, they are alive, active, and capable. What more should we ask for other than patience?

Of course, as adults, we don't stop growing either. We learn different things from our world, our children, and grandchildren. There are two things that I must remember when it comes to growth. One is that if I compare myself to those around me, it will stunt my growth as a person and the second is that I am still only passing through this world. *"For we are strangers before thee, and sojourners, as were all our fathers: our days on the earth are as a shadow, and there is none abiding."* 1 Chronicles 29:15

37. Ha Ha Ha

It's cold and wet outside and I can laugh at the weather. Why? Because I have so many things that will keep me warm. Warm drinks, soup, and home, these things help me to stay warm. I realise that not everyone is blessed with such comforts. Gratefulness is something that I don't exercise enough but I'm told that my quality of life would improve if I did.

1 Thessalonians 5:18 says *"In everything give thanks: for this is the will of God in Christ Jesus concerning you."* And I know just like me, that many people find this verse hard to comprehend particularly when they are in the middle of a crisis or bad patch. Yet it is there as a directive from God Himself.

From my experience, I have found that it is often only in hindsight that we can see the good that comes from those dark days when we wanted to yell, why me? instead of Thank You Lord.

Something else that I have discovered during my life, is that if we obey our Lord and Saviour, He will lead us down paths that will strengthen us and teach us things that we may never have learnt any other way.

Even when we are having a string of really bad days there will always be moments among them when we will be able to laugh at something or find some small thing to be grateful for. It might be a flower that has bloomed, a hug from a child, or just a nice hot cup of tea.

While it is hard to do, sometimes we just have to look at a situation from a different angle to see beauty, joy and happiness that we couldn't see before. On those bad days let us pray "God help me to see something beautiful, happy and lovely today".

38. Hands

We have a book that was given to my son when he was a baby. It's called "Two hands for helping". It explains that hands can do lots of things, such as do up buttons and stroke a cat, but the last line says: "and wave goodbye". The message here, I think, is to tell young children that sometimes we have to say goodbye to people. It won't always be goodbye forever but sometimes it will be.

How often do we have to wave goodbye to people and things? We may not physically stand and wave our hands when our material possessions are taken from us, but we have to let go and move on. We are only passing through this world and hanging on to all our goods will just clutter up our lives. They will weigh us down and restrict our freedom.

On the back cover of this little book, there is a chorus which finishes with: *"Two little hands to do His will and one little heart to love him still"*. This is what the hands that God gave us are for. They cannot do His will without our heart loving Him. Without this love what we do with our hands will be useless. *"If I gave everything I have to the poor and even sacrificed my body, I could boast about it; but if I didn't love others, I would have gained nothing."*
1 Corinthians 13:3

There are a lot of things that our hands can do that God needs our hands to work for Him. So, let us work hard and with love, for Him and for mankind.

37. Happy Place

I have two boys, these boys are like chalk and cheese; one is quiet, the other outgoing. One day when the boys were small, we were leaving the Post Office and one of them noticed the cross that could be seen on top of a church one block away. Why do churches put crosses on top of their buildings, he asked? To remind us that Jesus died so we can go to heaven was my response.

The outgoing one asked, "What is Heaven like?"

The quieter one responded with "A nice quiet peaceful place"

"Oh well, when I get there, I'll noise it up", was the comeback from his brother. I smiled and thought "Yeah, I'm sure you will".

As with my boys, one was happy when things were quiet and peaceful and the other was happy to be running around and investigating his world. Their ideas of Heaven were very different. No matter how many times I read the descriptions of Heaven in Revelation I have so much trouble being able to actually picture it. One thing is for certain, God tells us that: "And God shall wipe away all tears from their eyes; and there shall be no more death, neither sorrow, nor crying, neither shall there be any more pain: for the former things are passed away." Revelation 21:4

On an earthly level, I am in a happy place in front of my computer, connecting with people from all over the world. I learn lots about people from other countries, lifestyles and their struggles, dreams, and triumphs.

I'm just happy to connect with these people here on earth and I'm sure that some of them, I will be meeting for the first time in Heaven. Wow, what a happy place that will be!

40. I Bought This

Some years ago, I was given an ornamental pot plant holder. While it wasn't very big it still brightened up my lounge room. It was in the style of a classical Greek/Roman child holding an urn of some sort, into which the plant was supposed to go. However, like many of my things, it was knocked over one day and the urn part broke. The pieces that broke off were too small for me to glue back on and I have to admit that I really wasn't interested in doing that as I have never really had much success with patching china. I didn't feel like throwing the whole thing out, so it stayed in the corner in its broken state for some years – until I bought some artificial flowers to cover up the broken part.

You know, many people are broken, just like that ornament. Many people go out and buy all sorts of things to cover up their broken spirits. Things like make-up, new clothes, big homes, sports cars and even self-improvement courses, the list could go on and on. The truth is, they still often feel just as broken underneath.

When we read John 3:17 *"For God sent not his Son into the world to condemn the world; but that the world through him might be saved"* we are reading a promise from God to help those broken people. However, because we live in a broken world, there is a brokenness that will remain until we reach Heaven. Yes, we are saved, and Jesus has made something beautiful out of that brokenness but only in Heaven will we be completely healed. Isaiah 25:8 promises *"He will swallow up death in victory; and the Lord God will wipe away tears from off all faces..."*

41. I bought this on a Sunday!

As a child of Christian parents, I was taught that Sunday was a day of rest for everyone. Therefore, I find myself sometimes entering into a debate with myself about the rights and wrongs of shopping on Sundays. While it is obvious, that if we buy goods on Sunday, we are forcing others to work on Sunday. A minister once said we are happy to purchase a Newspaper on Monday morning, forgetting that in order for that paper to be available, staff have worked very hard on Sunday to make sure that it is available.

As we live out of town, I found it hard to keep enough food in the cupboards over the weekend while the children were attending school. It became necessary to purchase food after church on Sunday in order to have enough food for lunches on Monday.

A Christian friend once put it this way, "God allows acts of mercy to be carried out on Sunday and buying food for your children would be considered an act of mercy".

So, when buying things on Sunday, I am carrying out an act of mercy for those staff members who may not have sufficient hours to provide them with enough money to live on or no job at all.

While some may call this a bit of a stretch, Jesus carried out many acts of mercy for many people including healing a man with a crippled hand. Matthew 12:9-13. I pray that I will be a blessing by being cheerful when I buy.

42. I Found This...

"Grandma I found this car" the voice of my grandson breaks into my writing. He held out his hand and in his palm was the smallest car I have ever seen. It was such a small thing that it was no wonder that it had got lost in the first place. I'm surprised that it was even found. It reminded of some thoughts that I was having in the early hours of the morning; I was thinking about how small the cells are in our bodies and how they fit together to make us a whole person. Each cell has a different function and yet if we took it out of the body it would die and never work again.

This led me to thinking just how small we are, each of us, in the body of Christ. We are only one person, one in all those people that had faith in God from the beginning of time. Yet, no matter how small we feel and how insignificant we feel, God knows and loves us and will teach us in the unique way that He knows how. There will be times when we will feel lost and overwhelmed by the circumstances that we find ourselves in. Just like that small car that my grandson found we will be found by God and loved just as much as the person who is next to us as we drive along the road of life. "So, we, being many, are one body in Christ, and every one members one of another." Romans 12:5.

So often when I am struggling to understand where my life plan is going, I need to remember each cell is loved by my Heavenly Father.

43. I Hear

I hear home calling. My mobile phone rings and as I look at my phone and I can see that the call is coming from home. I have been away from home for several weeks now, I love being with other members of my family and they have looked after me so well while I have been sick, however, now that I am starting to feel better, I WANT TO GO HOME! I want to sleep in my own bed, watch my own television, eat from my own pantry, and see my own garden. (No, I won't be able to do anything, but still I just want to go home).

These things are familiar, they are mine and I want them around me again. When I was sick it didn't matter where I was, I just wanted to be cared for.

There is, of course, another home that one day will call to me. The desire to be there is of course very different to what I am experiencing right now. I have never been there; all I know about my real home is what I read in Revelation. I'm afraid my imagination just cannot put those words into any sort of picture that I can relate to. It is home to me because so many of my friends and family (particularly my mum) are already there waiting for me.

Besides, who wouldn't want to live in a perfect world, I know that I want to when my time comes. I also know that when I have completed the work that God has for me to do here, I will be ready to go home, but for the present, I'd like to say with Paul: *"For to me, to live is Christ and to die is gain. But if I am to live on in the flesh, this will mean fruitful labour for me; and I do not know which to choose."* Philippians 1:21-22.

44. I Never

I never thought I would become so disconnected from the world. Writing has been my connection with the outside world for a while now and suddenly I have lost my appetite for it. I have only been writing for a few years, but this is the first time that I have really not felt like writing at all. There has been no desire to even turn on the computer.

As I brought this to the Lord one morning I prayed about my serious lack of appetite and the response was if you eat what you are allergic to of course you are going to lose your appetite. This applies both physically and spiritually.

I've decided that I am allergic to bad, sad, and hyped up news. With the invention of social media, we have all become part of the news feed whether we like it or not. Regardless of the source: television, Facebook, or newspaper anything that falls into these categories needs to be avoided.

Now even I know that this is very unrealistic in today's world. We are force-fed this sort of information and unlike my physical allergies, which require me to take antihistamines. To stop me from dying, I cannot escape them.

What is the antihistamine for the bad news feed? It's found in Philippians 4:8 *"Finally, brethren, whatsoever things are true, whatsoever things are honest, whatsoever things are just, whatsoever things are pure, whatsoever things are lovely, whatsoever things are of good report; if there be any virtue, and if there be any praise, think on these things."*

We all have a responsibility to make sure that what we are dishing up is good food. As one lady I know constantly says PBIP (pray before I post).

45. In the Air

I was taking my first two flights on a large aeroplane. Even though I had taken several flights before, they had always been on a smaller aircraft. This one was big for me. On both occasions, I was seated behind the wings. Now what I found interesting was that when the plane was landing I could see some of the workings inside that wing. There seemed to be a lot of mechanical gear in there that we don't normally see on smaller aircraft. I was very aware that if one of those bits broke, we could be in a lot of trouble.

As I reflect on those journeys, I am amazed at the amount of faith that is placed in so many hands. There has to be faith in the mechanics who built the plane, faith that they did it correctly, faith in the maintenance crews and faith in the pilots who fly these monsters of the skies.

Yet ultimately, I had to place my faith, not in all these people but in God my father because He is the one that makes sure that all these people do the right things to make sure that the plane stays up in the air.

"And Jesus answering saith unto them, Have faith in God." Mark 11:22 after all *"Many are the plans in the mind of a man, but it is the purpose of the Lord that will stand."* Proverbs 19:21.

46. Joy

Joy is found in rare things. I do not mean rare things as in antiques or one-off productions. What I am thinking about are the rare things that happen every once in a while.

When I was a child, we only had fireworks once a year, on what we called Bonfire Night. We enjoyed it so much. These days' when fireworks are part of every function, show and festival, I find myself not enjoying them nearly as much. There was a time when life's little extras were given at birthdays and Christmas now, we have so many extras that we struggle to appreciate what we have, let alone find joy in them.

Christmas was special because you got to taste certain foods, drinks, and sweets. Easter time was a special time for Easter buns and chocolate. By making these things commonplace we remove their speciality and the joy of experiencing them once in a while.

I found joy recently in the birthday messages that I received from family and friends. They can only happen on my birthday and yes, they brought me joy. In times of drought, we experience joy when rain finally falls. It doesn't take long when it continually rains and floods for people to lose the joy of having rain. There is joy in being able to trust someone because these days' trust is something that is indeed special.

"Finally, there is only one God that cares for me, that I can trust and will never be ordinary so I find joy in Him. "Therefore, I tell you, do not worry about your life, what you will eat or drink; or about your body, what you will wear. Is not life more than food, and the body more than clothes?" Matthew 6:25.

47. Lighting

Different types of lights have a habit of making an object look different. When my husband wants to inspect a property, he likes to do it first thing in the morning because the afternoon sunlight always makes the grass appear greener, - strange but true! There are such a variety of lights available now. They all have a different purpose in that they will shed a different type of light in any room. If I want to read or work, I need a clear bright light, if I want to have a romantic setting, I am going to use dimmed lights or candles.

I believe there are times in our lives when God uses different types of lights to show us the way. On some occasions, He will use a strong clear light so that we can clearly see where we are to go and what we are supposed to do and yet other times He might use a dim light, one that makes us walk carefully, watching where we are going to put our feet down next.

It makes our lives very interesting and adds variety to our daily lives. I'm sure that if God used the same form of light for me each day, I would get bored and overconfident about what I was doing. God knows and understands that we need variety in our walk with Him. It also strengthens our faith to trust Him in very different situations.

"Your word is a lamp to guide my feet and a light for my path." Psalm 119:105.

Let's always walk carefully no matter what type of light we are walking in.

48. Looking In

I was thinking about when we finish looking in the mirror and walk away, we often forget what we saw. When enjoying the warmer Queensland weather during winter, I realise that I forget what it feels like to be cold. Our winters at home are very cold. Memory is an interesting thing, isn't it? Something can be locked away for many years and then for some reason it can resurface only to be gone all over again.

I think about my mum and the fact that she is in Heaven waiting for the rest of us to join her. While we are missing her, particularly at family events, I know that she would not want to return to earth. It's not that she wouldn't want to be at the wedding and celebrate with us, but she is having a better time, where she is.

Isaiah 65:16b says that *"because the former troubles are forgotten, and because they are hid from mine eyes"*. Just like I forget about the blemishes on my face when I walk away from the mirror and the cold at home, my mother has forgotten the troubles of this earth in Heaven. She will not have forgotten about her family and friends. She will be praying for them as she waits for us and that is the blessing of having a Godly parent.

Won't it be great to leave all our troubles behind when we move into our new home in Heaven!

47. Lucky Number

How fortunate (lucky) we are to have numbers in our lives. Of course, without numbers we would not be able to count musical notes, the days of the week, months of the year or even the years of history, money, people, account balances, the length of our lives, time, area, volume, and mass. When you start to think about numbers you realise that they are a very big part of our existence.

Without numbers, we cannot record the important things that happen in our lives and history. We can record the date we meet/marry our partners in life, my husband and I met on the 16th June 1977 and were married on the 7th January 1978. There are those all-important birthdays, 15th March, 24th March, 17th April, 22nd May, 5th June, 23rd September, 5th December to list but a few.

I remember trying to learn historical dates at school, interestingly enough, while I can remember the process, I cannot remember the actual dates of historic events. These events are also dated from a particular point in history when we started counting the years. This was the death of Jesus, the turning point in history which gives us BC and AD appendices to a date. Teachers would be out of work without numbers.

Eventually, there is going to be a place where numbers will not rule our lives because we will be living in a different dimension called eternity. "And there shall be no night there; and they need no candle, neither light of the sun; for the Lord God giveth them light: and they shall reign for ever and ever." Revelation 22:5.

As the famous songwriter says:
"When we've been there ten thousand years Bright shining as the sun. We've no less days to sing God's praise Than when we've first begun."

50. Making Mistakes

During a protracted family crisis, I was determined to try and not make any mistakes when it came to relating to other family members. As you no doubt guessed, yes, I made some. One night as I mulled over the mistakes, I'd made I moaned to God about how the people, particularly in the New Testament didn't make mistakes and why had I so easily fallen down. After all, they had the Holy Spirit to help them get it right.

God hit me over the head with this one. Of course, people in the New Testament made mistakes, they just don't look as bad to us because we could see how God had used those mistakes and worked His plan out anyway, regardless of the weakness of those humans that He had created. The only problem with my mistakes was that I couldn't see into the future. I cannot see how God was going to bring any good out of my bad.

I realised that this is another one of those faith things that we have to do. We have to do the best we can, understand that God is in control and He will do His work even though we let Him down time and time again. I really do need to take it to heart along with Paul in 2 Corinthians 12:9 which says *"And He said unto me, My grace is sufficient for thee; for my strength is made perfect in weakness. Most gladly therefore will I rather glory in my infirmities that the power of Christ may rest upon me."*

Yes, I will continue to make mistakes, but hopefully now, I will remember that God is bigger than anything I mess up.

51. Me Today

When I talk about who I am today, it always makes me think about who I was in the past. I have been a daughter, a wife, a young mum, a working mum, a stand-in mum, a housekeeper, teacher, volunteer, reader, gardener, a bookkeeper, a secretary, and a 'gofor' - that is probably not a real word but it was a real job. Above all these things I have been and still am today a child of God. He has used all the situations in my life, all the jobs that I have done and all the people that I have met to make me who I am.

So, what am I today that is different from my past? I am all these things still as well as being a writer. I love writing, so here I am sitting in my favourite spot, writing, and editing work on my computer. Some of it has been work that is developing over a period of weeks, some of it a month, those Minutes need to be checked before the next meeting on Wednesday and then there is today's story. There may even be more stories written if I find some source of inspiration.

I always pray that someone will be encouraged by what I write, why, because during my past I have needed lots of encouragement to become the person I am today. It's a case of wanting to thank those in my past by helping those in my present by passing it forward.

Romans 8:28 says: *"And we know that all things work together for good to them that love God, to them who are the called according to his purpose."* While I will not always manage to do what I intended, God is in control and He will work out His purpose.

52. Nature

What I like about Nature is its ability to recover from the devastating events that it's put through. Our Australian country is often subjected to horrific bushfires, winds, droughts, and floods. Even my garden is subjected to considerable periods of neglect from time to time depending on what other issues I have to deal with, and it still manages to bounce back to life once I start caring for it again.

So, what is the secret of this marvellous ability to recuperate? I can only point to an amazing God who created it in the first place. He did such a good job of creating the world that even He looked at what he made at the end of most days and declared that it was good. (Genesis 1)

Our man-made structures have no inbuilt ability to recover from destruction. Human hands must work hard to repair any damage. We may have to use a bulldozer and clear everything back to ground level and start again.

The other great thing is that we are also part of God's created wonders and when we are put through the storms of life, we can call on Him to help repair any bumps and bruises. *"And Jesus answering said unto them, they that are whole need not a physician; but they that are sick."* Luke 5:31. He promises that He will help us if only we ask Him in Jeremiah 33:3 *"Call unto me, and I will answer thee, and shew thee great and mighty things, which thou knowest not."*

So, each time I look around me and see the landscape recovering from a disaster, I can remind myself that the God of creation is so powerful that He is able and willing to help me through any of my tough times.

53. New

The first verses that come to mind this morning are Lamentations 3:22-23 "It is of the Lord's mercies that we are not consumed, because his compassions fail not. They are new every morning: great is thy faithfulness." The reason is because it is again raining here today. When we experience long periods of drought, it becomes a habit to get jumpy after more than a few days of dry weather. So, I'm thankful when God has been merciful and sent us more rain.

However, I am aware that maybe we stereotype what we believe "mercies" are. Do we think of mercies as always being good things, such as rain? Maybe mercies are also the dry spells in the weather, and our lives.

At this point, I am reminded of that saying: "Sometimes you have to be cruel to be kind" which I use when it is necessary to say "No" to children. We know that not every request our children present to us is good for them and so it's important for us to say that dreaded word "No".

Jesus says in Luke 11:13 "If ye then, being evil, know how to give good gifts unto your children: how much more shall *your* heavenly Father give the Holy Spirit to them that ask him?" We know that sometimes giving good gifts actually means withholding things from our children that may not be bad in themselves but inappropriate at their age and development. We have some idea of the consequences of giving some things to our children too early.

Now God knows us so much better, He also knows what the consequences will be simply because He can see the future and has planned it. So maybe those things we don't like might be new mercies that we just cannot see yet.

54. Nine O'clock

I was driving into town for a dental visit. On the way down the highway I noticed an ambulance parked on the side of the road. Ok someone in that house is very ill and I prayed for them. Not any great long prayer just what I call a Nehemiah prayer. Then I noticed two Police Officers standing talking to a couple. Alright, this is odd I thought. Then I finally pulled level with the next intersection and noticed glass on the road. "Oh, dear there has been an accident here, they really should do something about this corner, it is dangerous". Most locals know this and avoid it but sometimes you just can't.

What I didn't see, was my daughter, granddaughter, and her car on that corner. I had no idea that it was her that was involved in that accident until later that day when she rang me. This is the third accident that this family has experienced in less than a year, one of which took my mother's life and, in this case, if my daughter hadn't had the presence of mind to floor the accelerator the other driver would had hit my granddaughter square on. So, I am grateful for His protection of my family.

As I continued to thank Him for His protection at nine o'clock this morning I had to ask why? Not why were they involved in the accident but why didn't I see everything? I saw the police, ambulance, the other people but not my own family? She saw me drive past and it is as if they were hidden from my sight. It feels a bit like those situations when your children are very little, you are ten feet away and you see them starting to fall but you have no time to get to them in time to cushion their landing.

This question will be debated by me and God for a while yet, but the first response seems to be: "It doesn't matter how far away or how close you are; your children are in My hands now". Ecclesiastes 3:6 reminds me that there is: *"A time to get, and a time to lose; a time to keep, and a time to cast away;"* This doesn't mean that I am throwing away my family, but I do have to leave them in His care.

55. Old Plus New

I have a beautiful jug that I decided to use recently. However, when I cleaned it, I heard that annoying sound that told me that it had cracked. I picked it up, turned it around and eventually found the cracks. Some of the cracks were along the pattern so they were hard to see at first. My instinct was to throw it out. It was no longer any good as a jug. After all that is what it was made for, if it cannot be used as a jug, it is useless. Right! Well, maybe not? As I looked at it again, I saw that it was still pretty, it hadn't broken into a heap of pieces, sure it would no longer be able to hold water, but it could hold something. So, I recycled my jug.

As I was thinking about what to do with the jug, it also occurred to me that we, as human beings, are also cracked. We have all sinned; we are no longer the people that God created back in the Garden of Eden. Yes, some of our cracks may be hard to see by those around us but God can see them all. Yet, just as I love the jug, so God loves us more. Regardless of how broken we are or feel, He can still use us to bring glory to His name and we can still worship Him by doing what we can, working with what we have and carrying out those duties to the best of our abilities.

My jug now brings a new perfume into our house, it's full of Lavender, and it doesn't need to hold water, it just holds the lavender stalks. When we allow God to use us in whatever way He wants, we will bring a new fragrance into our world. No, we may not be doing what we were originally planned for, but we are still loved and cared for by our Lord and Saviour.

56. On the Wall

In our family room hangs a canvas photo that was taken during the driest time we have experienced during our time at Glenburnie Homestead. When I decided to get it printed my children objected on the grounds that we didn't need to be constantly reminded of how bad the country looked during that spell. They felt that the memories would be too depressing for their father who struggled back then. I consulted him before I went ahead, which meant that the print would no longer be the surprise that I wanted it to be.

He approved of the project on the grounds that photos are a snapshot in time. As he stated the only other aerial photo, we have shown the country looking green, but the green was thistles, not pasture.

The interesting thing about past memories, is that we often remember things to be better than they were. The Israelites did this when they were standing on the outskirts of the Promised Land. When faced with the challenges ahead of them, they forgot how hard life was back in Egypt.

When we look at this photo, we are reminded of how dry things were. We also remember how God took care of us during such a tough time. When we turn our eyes from the photo to the green pastures outside, we thank God for the rain that has fallen. It also makes us aware that things could get that bad again sometime in the future. Maybe when that time comes, we might do what Peter instructed us to do with more *confidence "Casting all your care upon him; for He careth for you."* 1 Peter 5:7, something I lacked last time. Hopefully, I have learnt this lesson.

57. Overwhelmed

There are times during our lives, that we can look around us and feel completely overwhelmed by the amount of work that we need to get through. The list can seem like a mass of water rushing towards us, threatening to drown us. We just feel as if we are never going to get through the challenges.

Like the extra water that floods a stream after a summer downpour and stays between its banks, our circumstances too, are confined by boundaries that God has set for us. Remember Job, a man who had to cope with so many disasters. God allowed Satan to give Job as much grief that he could handle without killing him. *"And the LORD said unto Satan, Behold, all that he hath is in thy power; only upon himself put not forth thine hand. So, Satan went forth from the presence of the LORD."* Job 1:12.

Now we must remember that we are not Job and God has completely different plans for each of us. So, when we are feeling overwhelmed, we can be reassured that God will not give us more than we can cope with. *"There hath no temptation taken you but such as is common to man: but God is faithful, who will not suffer you to be tempted above that ye are able; but will with the temptation also make a way to escape, that ye may be able to bear it."*
1 Corinthians 10:13.

At the times when we feel overwhelmed, we can have confidence that God has our best interests in mind and the lessons we learn will be part of His plan for us. *"And we know that all things work together for good to them that love God, to them who are the called according to his purpose."* Romans 8:28.

58. Path

It doesn't matter how many gardens you visit; they are all very different. What I like to look at, apart from the plants, in any garden is the different types of paths that they have. There is always such a different variety. They can be made of gravel, concrete, bricks, or pavers. I also like to investigate where the paths might lead because they often go in very different directions.

Our lives are also a bit like gardens, we have paths that go in very different directions to the others around us. All our paths go in different directions. It doesn't matter who we are or where we live, life will be a journey that will be different for each of us. Some journeys will be straight, long and with very few corners, like the great straight highways in the deserts. Others will have many corners, uphill grades, downhill runs, and others will be bumpy. The great designer designs each journey, the one that knows exactly who you are and what you will respond to best. He will lead you to a place where He has great work for you to do. Most likely you will not see a great work, but it will be because it is the job that He has planned for you and you are to affect someone in a very special way.

It doesn't matter where our journey takes us, what is important is that when we reach the end we will be able to say with Paul *"I have fought a good fight, I have finished my course, I have kept the faith: Henceforth there is laid up for me a crown of righteousness, which the Lord, the righteous judge, shall give me at that day: and not to me only, but unto all them also that love his appearing."* 2 Timothy 4:7-8.

No matter what the design is, let us all tread our paths faithfully.

51. Pink

In my garden, I have a Dahlia Tree. It is positioned in a protected corner behind the shed. They seem to flower very late in the season just about the time the frosts start to cover the ground some mornings. The plant grows high enough so the flowers can be seen only by looking up into the sky and so high light frosts don't kill them. It could be said that the flowers are up in the air.

As I enjoy the beauty of these flowers, I am reminded that my mother used to say that some Christians are so angelic, always up in the air harping, that they were of no earthly use. I know that high ideals and looking up are good things. It is also important that when it comes to relating to those people on the ground who are coping with the frosts of life, I need to be real and down to earth.

In Matthew 25:31-46 we read about how on judgement day God will separate the sheep from the goats. The sheep represent those people who have helped their fellow citizens by giving them food, clothes and shelter, very ordinary and necessary things for everyone to survive. These are the "down to earth" things that we are to do to help those who have found themselves out in the cold.

"And the King will say, 'I tell you the truth, when you did it to one of the least of these my brothers and sisters, you were doing it to me!" Matthew 25:40.

How we go about doing this will be different for each of us because we are individuals in the eyes of God, and we all have diverse talents. As we look up to Jesus, we can do some earthly good.

60. Pointy

Why do we make things pointy? In my experience, it usually means that we want to show people where to go. It is most likely related to the tradition of using our index finger to point to somewhere or someone. Of course, there is always the exception. Some pointy things are just for purely decorative purposes.

In the case of road signs, the point faces the direction you want people to go not where they have come from. If road signs did actually point you to where you had come from, they would be the most useless things in existence. You would be a very strange person if you did not know where you had come from.

When it comes to travelling our life's journey, Paul tells us not to look back while we are trying to move forward in life. *"Brethren, I count not myself to have apprehended: but this one thing I do, forgetting those things which are behind, and reaching forth unto those things which are before,"* Philippians 3:13. We all need to keep our eyes on where we are going, not where we have been.

What about the pointy structures on church buildings called steeples? These too, are meant to direct people to think about heavenly things, rather than earthly things. Paul encourages us to do this in Colossians 3:1-2 *"If ye then be risen with Christ, seek those things which are above, where Christ sitteth on the right hand of God. Set your affection on things above, not on things on the earth."*

There are signs that actually point in the wrong direction and if we follow them, we end up in the wrong place or completely lost. God however always knows where we are and can bring us home as soon as we ask.

61. Restore

When we try to fix things around our house we are trying, unsuccessfully, to restore things in line with the history of the house. We have unconfirmed reports that the house was built over one hundred years ago so must, of course, fix things in order to fit not only our lifestyle but also the social structure of the twenty-first century. The house has an unfinished look to it, but it has been remodelled in a way that has served us well, particularly when we had up to six children living here on a consistent basis. Mind you if the work is ever finished, I will most likely be a very old lady.

It is a bit like me. I'm not finished yet, I have my rough edges, faults and personality traits that could use some remodelling. God has started this massive job and He will continue to do so until the day He calls me home. *"For your fellowship in the gospel from the first day until now; Being confident of this very thing, that he which hath begun a good work in you will perform it until the day of Jesus Christ:"* Philippians 1:5-6.

No matter how long the house stands and no matter how many people will come and live in it, it will have different renovations and maintenance carried out to make sure that it stays standing. It needs to stay relevant to the living conditions of the families who will call it home. It could stand for a couple of hundred years yet, unlike me. My days are numbered by God, my father and I'm sure they will not be that long. *"For I know the thoughts that I think toward you, saith the LORD, thoughts of peace, and not of evil, to give you an expected end."* Jeremiah 29:11.

62. Rings

If there is a type of jewellery that I do like its rings. Necklaces tend to annoy me and earrings unless they are very good quality ones will make my ears sore. Yet my ring collection is not large.

The first ring that I received was my signet ring from my parents. I had just turned ten years old. I was growing up or so I thought, and the ring was to mark that milestone of life. I wore it so much that in the end, it wore out.

My next ring was a friendship ring from a boyfriend for my eighteenth birthday. That relationship didn't last and so I handed it back.

The next friendship ring I received was from the man who is now my husband, a month later I received an engagement ring and two months later my wedding ring. These rings all have various meanings and mark the different stages of our relationship. The friendship ring is engraved with a diamond pattern representing a lasting friendship. The engagement ring has a diamond which is supposed to mean "forever" and the wedding ring is a continuous circle of gold to signify a never-ending relationship.

The next important ring that I received was my fortieth birthday ring which I have named my prayer ring. This is because it has been set with a stone to represent each one of my children. When I look at my ring, I am reminded to pray for each one of them. This is of course not the only time I pray for them. My latest gift is my mother's dress ring given to me by my father just after her death.

Each time I look at my rings I am able to pray, remember or treasure the special people that God has brought into my life.

63. Scrambled Eggs

Sometimes I decide to make scrambled eggs for tea. It's an easy meal, and after a busy day, I am often not in a position to wait for meat and vegetables to cook. Often when I look at the yolks in the bowl, I notice that they often vary in colour.

Now some people would have you believe that the colour of the yolk is an indication of how healthy a bird is, but this is not the case. The colour of the yolks is determined by what they eat. If you feed a chook grass, they will be bright yellow. Regular chook feed bought from a store will not produce the bright yellow colour that some people desire in an egg. Sometimes it can also be related to the breed of a chook. It depends on which pen our chooks are in as to what diet they will have.

As I looked at the yolks, I thought about how we are all on different spiritual diets in our current world. Different preaches, internet posts and books give us the greatest variety in a spiritual diet this world has ever been able to partake of. These different diets will produce different levels of activity for the Lord. Some people have been encouraged from an early age and have the confidence to be upfront people, sharing their love of God with others. Others who have been discouraged, or abused, will still share their passion with others, but in a quieter manner behind the scenes. They are still all working hard for the Lord.

Yes, we may even look at our fellow Christians and judge them as being unhealthy, but that is not for us to decide. God is the one that feeds us daily. He is the one who will judge us at the end of time, and He is the one who we all have to answer too.

"As every man hath received the gift, even so minister the same one to another, as good stewards of the manifold grace of God." 1 Peter 4:10.

The colour of my egg yolks doesn't matter once they are mixed together. I cannot tell which egg yolks were pale and which were bright yellow, but I have made a great meal. When we all work together, we will be able to expand the kingdom of God greatly and the colour of our talents won't matter. God will be pleased with the healthy way we have all worked together.

64. Season

There are four seasons in a year, and while it might be summer here in the southern hemisphere it is winter in the northern hemisphere. I think about our men who went to war from Australia, leaving our shores in one season and arriving in the opposite season when they disembarked from the ships.

As I watch the television and the news about the storms, I remember a story that my mother told me about waking up in the middle of the night during a storm. She was frightened, but there was her father standing beside her bed. She jumped into his arms and he was able to cuddle her and calm her down.

As I turned this story over in my mind it occurred to me that the reason that he was already there may have been because the noise of the storm had woken him and invoked memories of the war. So, feeling a little disturbed himself he was aware of the fears that his child might experience.

This story also reminds me of another father who is always there, waiting for us to come to Him for comfort when we are afraid. His disciples were very afraid during a terrible storm on the Sea of Galilee and yet Jesus walked out to be with them and comfort them; *"And when the disciples saw him walking on the sea, they were troubled, saying, It is a spirit; and they cried out for fear. But straightway Jesus spake unto them, saying, Be, of good cheer; it is I; be not afraid."* Matthew 14:26-27.

So today as I remember a soldier, Robert Archibald Deans, I remember a man who even after he came home, had the courage to put his fears aside and stepped out to help and comfort those going through a stormy season.

65. Skyline

When it comes to viewing the skyline from my house, I am absolutely spoilt for choice. You see if I walk around my house, there are only a few places where structures obscure my skyline. At any point, I can see mountains, valley's, trees, and a vast sky that goes on forever.

The first passage that comes to mind is Psalm 121 *"I look up to the mountains—does my help come from there? My help comes from the LORD, who made heaven and earth! He will not let you stumble; the one who watches over you will not slumber. Indeed, he who watches over Israel never slumbers or sleeps. The LORD himself watches over you! The LORD stands beside you as your protective shade. The sun will not harm you by day, nor the moon at night. The LORD keeps you from all harm and watches over your life. The LORD keeps watch over you as you come and go, both now and forever."*

God has definitely been there for me. As each hollow and mountain has been moved through or climbed, He has proven that He has the answers worked out well in advance. He has sent the right person at the right time or just given me the energy, motivation, and strength to get through the list of things to be carried out.

No matter where I look, I can see mountains. So, no matter where I look, I am reminded that God not only made these wonderful formations, but He will care for me. He cares for me, a very, very small speck on the surface of His great creation.

As I look forward to the future, I know that those mountains are going to still be there proving God's faithfulness.

66. Snack

So, what did our soldiers in World War One eat? From what I have been told, Beef Jerky was something that was common. My son has decided that he likes this snack which has no doubt been improved and certainly I understand that the packaging has.

I'm sure that those soldiers would be surprised that this is a snack that is appreciated by the younger generations. I know from personal experience that when you have no choice about what you have to eat and it is the only food available for an extended period of time you get to the stage where you really can't look at it without feeling sick. After all, facing that particular food again will bring back memories of when you had no choice but to eat it. Our soldiers would not be able to associate good memories with Beef Jerky.

As adults, there are a lot of things that we have no choice about doing. This is something that is impossible for young children to understand. It often comes as a shock to young adults, as they realise that there are certain things that just have to be done regardless as to how you feel about it.

Many of these young men were given no choice about going to war but they were adult enough to step up to the plate and do what had to be done for the loved ones at home and all future generations, to come.

Snacks are meant to be something you eat in order to get to the next meal but many of these men had to survive on these snacks alone.

As we remember our soldiers, I have to ask myself, would I have the courage and determination that all these people showed.

Do not forget their sacrifice.

67. So this happened!

The door has become unhinged! While working in the bedroom the other day, I wondered why the door of the wardrobe would not stay closed. This was part of the first bedroom suite we purchased just before our marriage in 1978. We had to carry out a few repairs in the first year or so but since then it has been moved each time, we changed houses and stood up to the abuses of five children and numerous grandchildren. So, I wasn't surprised when I discovered that the door had come unhinged? You see I knew that the hinge was getting loose and I didn't do anything to fix it.

Thinking about this, I wondered if many people think that society is a little bit the same way – unhinged. What does it mean to be unhinged anyway? It means that things don't work properly. I ask you, is our society working properly? Do we care enough about people to respect their property? Some people do, absolutely, but those who rob and destroy, don't. Do we care enough about people being abused? Some do, but those who use violence against their fellow man, women, and children, here at home and overseas, don't. Do we look out for each other? Some do but those greedy people who take from the poor just to make themselves rich, don't.

Yes, I think that our society is a bit like that wardrobe door, it is unhinged. How did it get like that? Most likely in much the same way as that wardrobe door. We failed to notice that it was falling apart, or if we did, we were too busy to do anything to fix it.

How do we fix our society then? That is easy *"Thou shalt love thy neighbour as thyself..."* Leviticus 19:18.

68. Something Green

As the rains fell, our paddocks were transformed from being boring brown in colour to bright green and covered in feed. It didn't happen overnight, but it felt a bit like it. It happened because my husband had put in a lot of money and hard work before the rains came. Of course, without the rain, no transformation would have happened.

I was thinking about transformations after I woke from my first dream last night. The magic of dreams can be so amazing! In a dream, people who have died are suddenly alive and well, bad relationships no longer exist, and our world can be transformed into something that is perfect. However, we all eventually have to wake up and face the real world. We remember those loved ones have died, the bad relationship is still not right, and our world is exactly the same as it was the night before if not a little more painful.

The truth is real transformations can happen, but they don't happen overnight and not without a lot of hard work. Even when we come to Christ to be saved and transformed, we start out on a long, hard, and often difficult journey. *"And be not conformed to this world: but be ye transformed by the renewing of your mind, that ye may prove what is that good, and acceptable, and perfect, will of God."* Romans 12:2. This journey will take a lifetime.

There is only one transformation that will happen in an instant. That is the one that will happen when we go home to be with our Heavenly Father. In an instant, my broken body will be transformed into a new body and I will be in a new world, a perfect world that is beyond my imagination and for once it will not be a dream.

61 Something White

I only drink white tea or soda water. So today my something white is my white tea that I had when I was able to share some time with a friend. It may not seem very special to you, but for the two of us, this was special. She lives on one side of town and I live on the other. So, for weeks now we have been planning this event. Each time we set a date, things go wrong, either she has gotten sick, or I have.

So, you may think that today's plan finally worked but you would be wrong. You see today, neither of us was planning on going to town. I only went to town because I decided that I wanted some craft supplies. When I was getting in the car, I remembered that I had some old medical supplies that needed to be taken to our Chemist. They had only been in the car for a week! As I walked into the Chemist my friend was there talking, so I didn't interrupt them. Walking out I commented to God that if we were to have that cuppa today than it would be up to Him to arrange.

As I walked back past the Chemist from another store, I almost expected to meet them walking out the door but no there was no sign of my friend. I crossed the street and was getting into my car when my friend emerged from the shop. I watched to see where she was going and soon realised that I had parked my car right next to hers. I waited and we had that cuppa.

"The preparations of the heart in man, and the answer of the tongue, is from the LORD." Proverbs 16:1.

70 Sparrows

Around our home, we have a particular bird that tends to create a lot of mess. They are a wonderful host for these horrid things called lice. Some people consider them to be only a pest.

Yet, they are special to God, so special that they are specifically mentioned in the Bible at least five times. Yes, they are sparrows. "Are not five sparrows sold for two cents? Yet not one of them is forgotten before God." Luke 12:6. It has been suggested that we need to try and get rid of them, but I know that we cannot get rid of them without putting all the other small birds at risk.

1 Timothy 2:3-4 *"For this is good and acceptable in the sight of God our Saviour; Who will have all men to be saved, and to come unto the knowledge of the truth."* This verse tells us that Jesus came to earth to make salvation available to everyone. Not just the good people, not just the rich people, not just the people of one nationality, He came to save all mankind and yes that includes women and children as well.

Do you feel like a sparrow, useless and pest like, **well guess what!** Jesus came to save you and you are so special to Him. Come to Him today, He will accept you, mess, and all; He loves you just the way you are.

"For God so loved the world, that he gave his only begotten Son, that whosoever believeth in him should not perish, but have everlasting life." John 3:16

We are all as special as sparrows.

71. Starts with Rope

We have a lawnmower that is well over twenty years old. It is showing signs of its age. It's rough and ready and it STARTS WITH A Rope. It has trouble getting started some mornings, particularly after it's been on holidays due to wet weather or it has been waiting for the grass to grow. On these occasions, I have to enlist the help of "Aerostart" and either my husband or son's muscles. When it goes, it does a very good job.

This lawnmower reminds me of myself, some days. I'm a bit rough and ready and battered. I have trouble getting started more mornings than I care to admit. I'm showing quite a few scars and wrinkles of life. The most wonderful thing is, that like my mower I am still useful to God. Even if I was completely broken physically (bedridden), I would be able to lie here and pray all day and God could use that. He heard the prayers of a bedridden lady in England in 1872 and sent a revival through the preaching of D L Moody. (Christian Preachers, Nigel Clifford p291) I'm not bedridden, however, and yes, if you get me fired up, I can still move a mountain of work. Mind you – afterwards I need to rest to get over it. We are instructed to be: *"Not slothful in business; fervent in spirit; serving the Lord; Rejoicing in hope; patient in tribulation; continuing instant in prayer;"* Romans 12:11-12. There are three things to remember about what we do for the Lord:
1: It's what He wants us to do;
2: that we do it with all our heart, soul, and mind and,
3: it's for His glory, not ours.

No, we don't need rope to get us started but let's rest in Him and start anyway.

72. Starts with "S"

One morning I had to face a sink full of dirty dishes. I'd had a busy day or two and I just could not face the dishes from last night. As I worked my way through the mountain I prayed. I prayed for a young family who were facing grief again. I prayed for the meeting I had the next day. I prayed that God would give me a sense of humour for when I had to face some "big people" in my life. I thanked God for the other authors and friends who had encouraged me during my very busy couple of weeks. I also thanked him for the lack of panic that I was feeling, even though I was feeling muddled headed and unmotivated.

As the mountain of dishes dissolved my thoughts turned to how quickly things get done when we stop messing around and just start the job that is in front of us.

In the past, I have often asked my children to do something and their cry has been but that's just too big for me to do. Yet the job has always been accomplished when they have tackled it, one toy, one article of clothing or one piece of rubbish at a time.

I was discussing a project with someone recently, and they commented that they would only be able to carry it out if everything fell into place. My response was that it doesn't work like that. The only way to make it happen is to put things in place so that they could do what they wanted. What do they say? A journey of a thousand miles starts with a single step, but if we don't take that first step, we will be forever at the starting line. Of course, we must not plan without asking God to guide us along the way.

73. Starts with "T"

Most of my days start with a cup of Tea. I am often woken by my husband with my first cuppa of the day even if he is going off to work. There are varying opinions on how good or bad this drink is for us but I know that I feel better after having one. Most people who know me have a good stock on hand for when I come to visit.

The other thing that I should do, first thing in the morning, is delve into the word of God, or to at least have a conversation with Him to get my day off to a good start.

When I do:

He Teaches me about His desires for me, *"Teach me thy way, O LORD; I will walk in thy truth: unite my heart to fear thy name."* Psalm 86:11

He Enlightens me about where He would like me to go and what He would like me to do *"Thy word is a lamp unto my feet, and a light unto my path."* Psalm 119:105.

He Assures me of my salvation in Christ *"Truly, truly, I say to you, whoever hears my word and believes him who sent me has eternal life. He does not come into judgment, but has passed from death to life."* John 5:24

So, when you start your day with a cup of TEA just remember that God would like to join you, teach, enlighten, and assure you as well.

74. Strange

It might seem strange, that a person would light a wood stove in the middle of summer. Yet, I have lit the stove three times this week. Why? Thunderstorms are a big part of our Australian summers and often when they get wound up our electricity gets cut off. The wood stove allows us to indulge in a hot meal and hot drinks while we wait for those poor workers suffering in the stormy weather to reconnect us.

I was advised on many occasions to dispose of our wonderful pieces of history and go all electric. I refused, I insisted on keeping our high tank, which gravity feeds water through our taps, along with our wood stove. This amazing high tank watering system is currently out of action as the tank has developed a hole which gravity feeds water straight out on to the ground, faster than through our taps. This means that we are currently dependent on electricity to make sure that our house has a constant water flow. But the wood stove is still sort of functioning. Once it would have heated our water as well, but that system got clogged and no longer works. It will however still cook a decent meal and boil water hotter than the electric jug, so I rejoice in that much.

As our technology advances and gets more elaborate, it will be harder to hang onto what is considered old fashioned technology. I see no need to dispose of such equipment; it works effectively and is really much greener than people give it credit for.

There is a saying that goes along the lines of its not wise to put all your eggs in the one basket and I would agree. This is my effort at doing just that.

75. Stripes

I went to the pantry cupboard the other day and discovered that there were two packets of Candy Canes left over from Christmas. These sweets are made of red, white, and sometimes green hard candy stripes twisted together in a spiral pattern. Finally, they are shaped to look like a walking cane or shepherds crook before being packed for sale.

There is a story that says the original candy canes were made to remind all of us that; Jesus is our Shepherd who loves and cares for us, shed His blood (red) for us. *"I am the good shepherd: the good shepherd gives his life for the sheep."* (John 10:11) This means that he can take away our sins and present us as pure as snow (white) to His father on judgement day. *"In the body of his flesh through death, to present you holy and unblameable and unreproveable in his sight:"* (Colossians 1:22). His promises and faithfulness are everlasting (green). *"Jesus Christ is the same yesterday and today and forever."* (Hebrews 13:8). This sweet was made with hard candy to remind us that Jesus has a strength that is stronger than anything we know. *"I can do all things through Christ which strengtheneth me."* (Philippians 4:13).

So when I look at the candy canes left in my cupboard, I am reminded how much Jesus loves us all and remember what Isaiah 53:5 says: *"But he wounded for our transgressions, he was bruised for our iniquities: the chastisement of our peace was upon him; and with his stripes we are healed."*

What a wonderful thing to remember every day.

76. Summer/Winter

In Australia, we have summer while friends in the northern hemisphere have winter. The earth here is busy producing lots of growth in the warm weather and sunshine. We are also celebrating this year as we have actually had some decent rain for the first time in many years. I know that on the other side of the earth everything is resting; plants are hibernating, waiting for spring to come. Genesis 8:22 assures us that *"As long as the earth remains, there will be planting and harvest, cold and heat, summer and winter, day and night."*

I guess God knew us well enough to know that we would not rest unless we were forced to. This would be why He designed winter's shorter days, forcing us inside much earlier than during the long days of summer. Personally, I find winter a nice time of the year. I love being curled up in front of a heater with a good book to read or writing more stories.

These days many people try to tell us that "Mother Nature" is responsible for controlling the weather and seasons. "They do not say from the heart, *"Let us live in awe of the LORD our God, for he gives us rain each spring and fall, assuring us of a harvest when the time is right."* (Jeremiah 5:24). God made them all and we should honour Him, even when the weather brings problems to be dealt with such as droughts, storms, and floods.

It is His inspiration that enables us to work out how to live within the boundaries that the weather permits us. So, we have worked out how to heat or cool our homes and the development of plants that grow within the confines of short summers or very cold winters. To God be the glory.

77. Sun

It's late afternoon and the sun is shining in through my window. The room glows with a brightness that only the sun can create. As I looked at the window, I noticed just how dirty it was. I realised that the dirt was more noticeable because the sun was behind it, if I had drawn the curtains against the cold winter weather, I would have been able to hide the mess. If I had, of course, the room would have been plunged into a dreary darkness.

It occurred to me that our lives are like my window. Dirty with sin. Yet it takes Jesus, the Son of God and the Holy Spirit who shine on it, for us to see it. I had to smile at the differences between the effects of the Sun on my window and God's Son on my life. That sun shining through my window wasn't going to be able to clean it. It would only bake that dirt on more and make it harder to clean off. While Jesus the Son of God will clean my life of dirt and shame if I would only ask Him.

Yes, I can draw the curtains on my life and ignore the sin that is there. I can cover it up with explanations of "I'm human", "I'm not perfect" or "I'm just busy". But sooner or later God is going to pull those curtains back and He is going to say "Look child I want to help you see a better way, a nicer room, a clearer, brighter view of the world".

"Come now, and let us reason together, saith the LORD: though your sins be as scarlet, they shall be as white as snow; though they be red like crimson, they shall be as wool." Isaiah 1:18.

Are you willing to pull back the curtains of your life and let God's son brighten it?

78. Super Results

We are sowing our paddocks on faith today. We have had about three inches of rain. The ground is not soaking wet, but it is damp enough to get things started. We are moving into Summer and we are going to need feed for our stock. My husband went out and purchased "Super" and "Super Dan" seed and planting is underway.

Super is the fertilizer that will help the seeds to get a good start in life. Super Dan is the name of the grass that will, if all things go well, give us enough feed for our stock or to make hay. It would be easy to think that with all this "super" stuff, we will end up with a "super" amount of feed. However, it will be the ordinary things such as sunshine and rain that will ensure a bumper crop.

So, it is with us. It doesn't matter what sort of start you have in life, you may be born with the best privileges and advantages that society can offer, but you won't necessarily make a success of your life. It will be the ordinary things such as love, care, understanding and good choices that will enable most children to make a grander contribution to our society.

Once you have made the most of the resources around you, you can only rise up in faith and move forward one step at a time. The results will then be up to God and He will work it out even if we don't get the results that we would like. We have no guarantees that this crop is going to be successful, but if we have carried on in what we consider to be a sensible manner. We know we have done our best. If it fails, we still trust God to look after us in the future.

77. Superannuation

Superannuation funds are paid into by employers on behalf of their workers, so that they will have funds to live on when they retire. These funds have to be paid on a weekly basis and add to the costs of employing staff. It is the obligation of the fund owner to make sure that there is an increase in these monies by responsible investments. There are a great number of these funds in Australia and they do perform at differing rates of success. What reserves people have available when they retire will depend on just how well these funds perform. Staff members are also able to sacrifice part of their salaries to add to these funds. It is a means of storing up funds against a future need.

While it is a sensible thing to do in order to try and prevent workers being dependent on Government pensions, it is still a material good that can be eroded by the fall of stock markets and bad performances of investments.

Matthew 6:19-21 warms us to *"Don't store up treasures here on earth, where moths eat them and rust destroys them, and where thieves break in and steal. Store your treasures in heaven, where moths and rust cannot destroy, and thieves do not break in and steal. Wherever your treasure is, there the desires of your heart will also be."*

That is not telling us to be silly when it comes to business practices but it is telling us to remember that in the end all things on earth will eventually rot away and we are not able to take anything into eternity with us. We cannot force people to follow Jesus but if we share the gospel and carry out acts of kindness that help others make that choice, then we are laying up treasure in Heaven.

80. Sweet

How sweet are childhood memories for some of us? They were times when we were protected, unconcerned with the rights or wrongs of the world and enjoyed very few responsibilities. I know that not everyone enjoyed such lives, but I was blessed with such a childhood and I am grateful for such a start in life.

Those good memories are a place I go to when I am feeling tired, stressed, and frustrated with adulthood. When late night phone calls give you cause for concern, illness and pain keeps you awake into the early hours of the morning and you need a good place to go, in order to distract yourself. My childhood memories are that place for me.

Do you remember thinking that adults could do as they pleased? I do. Even my children accused me of this privilege. Adult life has a habit of handing you a great number of responsibilities, all of which we are totally unaware of as children. I am sure we all have days when all these things weigh heavily on us, and we would love to be children again. We don't want to deal with the constant stream of duties. *"When I was a child, I spoke and thought and reasoned as a child. But when I grew up, I put away childish things."* 1 Corinthians 13:11, but some days we wish we didn't.

When we have one of those days, it seems hard to understand what God would like us to do. 1 Corinthians 13:12 seems very relevant *"Now we see things imperfectly, like puzzling reflections in a mirror, but then we will see everything with perfect clarity. All that I know now is partial and incomplete, but then I will know everything completely, just as God now knows me completely."*

Thank goodness one day I will see clearly what sweet plans God has for me.

81. Teaching Myself

There have been many times during my life when I knew that I had to teach myself something new. It could have been something as simple as breaking an old habit or disposing of emotional and spiritual baggage. It could also be something new like writing. The best method I have found that works for me is repeating it. It's an old-fashioned strategy. This method of teaching was used in schools when my mother was a girl. Children were taught such things as their Times Tables and spelling by what is now known as "Rout". This was achieved by the students saying them over and over again until they were permanently imprinted in the mind.

While I wouldn't recommend this for every learning experience, it does work sometimes. I have found that for myself when I begin the learning exercise, I remind myself that I only have to do this differently this once. Not forever, just this once. This stops me thinking that I am trying to change to the habit forever and it is too hard and unattainable. It makes the target, this once, attainable, and achievable. If I do this every time, I have found that I eventually end up doing things the new way as a matter of habit.

In the Old Testament, the Israelites were instructed to do the law of God constantly every day and to tell their children about the wonders of God. This was so they would remember who their God was, how wonderful He was and how He wanted them to live their lives.

If I take this principle and ask God to help me break an old habit one very small step at a time, then I am moving forward in faith and that is all He wants us to do.

82. Testing, Testing, Can You Trust Me?

Imagine walking along a beach, you look out and watch the waves roll over the rocks, turning around, you see the cliffs of sand that have been carved out to make the beach that you are now enjoying. However, the most interesting things are the shells and rocks that are scattered across the sand.

The thing is that amongst those rocks and shells (particularly in Australia) you sometimes come across a pretty blue creature. It is so pretty, that there is a temptation to pick it up and examine it. However, if you do, you will regret it. These creatures have a sting that will make you very sick for a very long time. Life can sometimes be like walking along a beach, things are good, there are very few problems and yet there is always that small niggling sin that we can be tempted to pick up and play with.

I see God testing me to make sure that I trust Him to be faithful. I have three books to my name and enough material to have three or four more. I know that there are at least two other authors with the same name as my own. Yet, as I see their advertisements on my computer, (they must be able to afford such a thing) and I see the success of other authors it would be very easy for me to pick up that little blue bottle of jealousy, how can God give these people more success than me? Yet, each time those thoughts enter my head I must sidestep them, push them away or else I am going to be stung. If I don't, I will suffer and suffer dearly. God is asking me to trust Him in a way that He has not asked me before and if I am careful, I will see His great hand work in such a way that I have never seen before.

"Many, O LORD my God, are thy wonderful works which thou hast done, and thy thoughts which are to us-ward: they cannot be reckoned up in order unto thee: if I would declare and speak of them, they are more than can be numbered." Psalm 40:5.

83. This is Good

Some traditions are good, but of course they may not be good for everyone. At Easter, we remember that Jesus died on the cross and rose again to save us from our sins. Just like birthdays, Anzac Day, and Christmas we have special traditions here in Australia that help us remember and celebrate. Other countries have their traditions which are often different to ours.

On Good Friday, we have the tradition of eating Hot Cross Buns, because they remind us of the cross and what Jesus did there for us. We have traditionally eaten Lamb for dinner as this reminds us that Jesus was the Lamb of God, the perfect sacrifice for our sins. It was also more convenient as we have always been sheep graziers. "For if by one man's offence death reigned by one; much more they which receive abundance of grace and of the gift of righteousness shall reign in life by one, Jesus Christ." Romans 5:17.

We have never been big fish eaters in our family. However, we have had fish on the table at times to remind us that Jesus wants us to go out and tell others about why He died for all mankind. *"Go ye therefore, and teach all nations, baptizing them in the name of the Father, and of the Son, and of the Holy Ghost:"* Matthew 28:19.

While these things are good to help us remember the events of Good Friday what really is important is that we remember the Word of God in our hearts. If we cannot celebrate any day without the trappings, then they are occupying a place they were never intended for. I no longer can eat Hot Cross Buns, but I never have to celebrate Good Friday without knowing scripture and that is a good thing.

84. This Smells so Good

My husband took me out for dinner one night. This is something we don't do very often and only at selected places that can accommodate my food issues. While we were waiting for our order, I had a conversation with the waitress about why I cannot drink coffee.

My children can and so each time I open a tin of coffee I smell the aroma and it smells so good. The trouble is that if I was to actually drink a cup of coffee I wouldn't feel nearly as good as it smells. With these thoughts came thoughts about how so many of our advertisers work on the principle of "if it feels good, do it". The hope is, that people will buy in order to make themselves feel good. Then when that doesn't work, they will continue to buy more and more things, looking for that good feeling.

It is very common to take the easy way out. If the coffee didn't actually make me very sick, there is no way I would be able to resist the temptation to drink some. I won't reveal how many cups of coffee a day I used to drink but it was a lot.

Resisting temptation is sometimes made easier by being afraid of the consequences, but in these days of "the feel good" approach, too many people are not afraid of them and are even willing to simply deal with them.

Sooner or later we will have to deal with them anyway. As we read in Revelation 20:15 *"And whosoever was not found written in the book of life was cast into the lake of fire."* This isn't just about resisting temptation of course but also about failing to take God at His word that if we ignore the sacrifice of Jesus there will be consequences.

85. Three Things

One January 25th I collected some roses, red for love, pink for joy and white for peace. As we celebrated Australia Day that day, I knew that what our country needed more than ever, are those three things: Love, Joy and Peace.

So many people try to find these things in different ways. Some people try to find love in relationships that end badly and are often only instigated through a blur of hurt. There are those that try to find joy in what they do, working hard, being the best, playing sport or shopping until they drop. Finding peace, well many try to crawl away and hide while others use drug induced sleep to try and help. But it doesn't work!

On a state, federal and global level, governments also try to make these things a reality. They try to generate love by having conferences, where leaders are supposed to talk and come to agreement over many different issues. Joy is supposed to be created when they spend great sums of money on sporting events such as the Olympic, Commonwealth and Asian Pacific games. To make peace all they seem to do is make economic or military war. But it's just not working!

We need to accept Love – *"Greater love hath no man than this, that a man lay down his life for his friends."* John 15:13.

We need to absorb Joy – *"These things have I spoken unto you, that my joy might remain in you, and that your joy might be full."* John 15:11.

We need to receive Peace - *"Peace I leave with you, my peace I give unto you: not as the world giveth, give I unto you. Let not your heart be troubled, neither let it be afraid."* John 14:27.

Jesus can give us these three things and IT WORKS!!!

86. 'Tis the Season to

'Tis the season to learn about the real meaning of Christmas. It seems that commercialisation of Christmas encourages those selfish desires in each of us that create disharmony and stress. There is so much advertising hype that makes people feel as if nothing is good enough. Advertisers continue to bombard us with messages to entice us to outdo everyone else.

Yet, what is Christmas all about? It is supposed to be about good tidings, goodwill to all men and joy to the world. That first Christmas was about so many unselfish acts. The first one being that Mary accepted the miracle of carrying the Son of God regardless of what family and friends would think of her. Today, we don't frown when we come across a single mother. We encourage and support her, realising that mistakes can be made. In the society that Mary grew up in you could be killed for being a single mother and who on earth was going to understand an immaculate conception. Joseph unselfishly put aside his feelings and desires to look after Mary and Jesus, again regardless of how weak and stupid others saw him. In Bethlehem the Inn Keeper unselfishly allowed Mary and Joseph to use the stable. It's hard to believe that this is a remarkable act but if the Inns were arranged the way I understand them to be; with everyone sleeping on mats around the walls in the same room then his willingness to arrange some form of privacy for her indicates to me an unselfish man. The wise men travelled a great distance and gave gifts.

Goodwill and Joy are born out of the unselfishness of humans towards each other. Let's teach our children the real meaning of Christmas so that its spirit will be felt all year round but especially at Christmas time.

87. Today I Saw...

My granddaughter is quite talented, she is nearly six years old and while I could be considered biased, I can see potential. It is raw and childlike but then the artist is only a child herself. If the raw talent is nurtured, practised and developed, then one day I could be attending an art gallery featuring her work. This is, of course, just speculation and no one can predict what the future holds for this wonderful little girl, she will face many challenges and situations which will all shape her destiny in one way or another.

She reminds me of how our lives as Christians can be like her art. No matter how old we are when we come to Jesus and start our walk with Him, our faith is raw and childlike. It needs to be nurtured, practised, and developed so that it will grow into something beautiful for the world to see. It will be able to pass on messages of love, patience, and encouragement to those who see the growth that takes place. Yes, its growth will be determined by the challenges and situations, both good and bad, that the person has to go through, but the hand of God will always be there to guide and direct them. The big difference here is that while I cannot see what is in my granddaughter's future, God can, and He sees all our futures.

"Neither is there any creature that is not manifest in his sight: but all things are naked and opened unto the eyes of him with whom we have to do." Hebrews 4:13.

"If I ascend up into heaven, thou art there: if I make my bed in hell, behold, thou art there." Psalm 139:8 and that is no speculation.

88. Too Much

I have too much mess. Our bathroom has a curtain which hangs in front of an old-fashioned vanity unit. This curtain conceals a mountain of dust, dirt, and objects. As I cleaned it up, I found all sort of things that had been hidden from public view. It was hard work and I am ashamed to admit just how long it has been since I last made an effort to clean it. I found a pair of earrings that I missed not long ago and hidden there by one of my children. A football belonging to my now grown son was also unearthed along with pegs, a corn fork, and a needle.

As I swept, scrubbed, washed, and sorted the mess I thought about how we hide things from public view. We can cover our fears, our anger, and disappointments from others, particularly if we are careful to present a happy and confident front when we are out and about.

However, there is that one person we cannot hide from, no matter how hard we try. God sees all our tears, fears, joys, and achievements. He sees everything, right down to those thoughts we like to keep to ourselves.

"If I ascend up into heaven, thou art there: if I make my bed in hell, behold, thou art there." Psalm 139:8. Yes, you may not see everything that I do but God does! It doesn't matter how many faults I have right now because He is working on me. He is cleaning, sweeping, and sorting me out. It is a process that will take as long as I live. It will be ongoing, and one day it will be complete. On that day I will go to be with Him and know that it has all been worth the hard work.

89. Tradition

In our western society there almost always seems to be a fear of tradition. Maybe it is because we see them as being tight and inflexible. It was something that my sister and I discussed while I stayed with her during the week leading up to the anniversary of my mother's death.

I remember years ago, reading a story about a young widow feeling very frustrated, because the tradition of wearing black for mourning had been done away with. It wasn't that she didn't believe her husband was in heaven or that she had no hope of seeing him again, but the fact was that her life was not the same and she wanted some way to tell people that, she was hurting without having to explain it in words.

I have a personal tradition of wearing a particular top to funerals, not because there is no hope for those that have passed away but because there is a dark time in front of those left behind. The top is black and white, white which represents the purity of God's love and black for the darkness of our lives without our loved ones.

As we read through the Bible, we see that there were many traditions that the Jews held on to, and yes, the spirit of these events was often abused. Jesus had a bit to say about them, but He also told us to observe some traditions as well. *"And he took bread, and gave thanks, and brake it, and gave unto them, saying. This is my body which is given for you: this do in remembrance of me."* (Luke 22:19) just to name one.

Let us be careful not to throw away traditions altogether because they are to remind us of the goodness of God.

90. Trash

One man's trash is another man's treasure, so the saying goes. Thinking about where I would be able to find some trash in a very well kept and clean house was a challenge. The only thing I could think of was the compost heap in the back yard. Here we have the classic theme that I keep coming back to. A compost heap is made up of weeds, rubbish, and garden waste, which is mixed together and left to break down and change into a product that can then be returned to the garden to revitalise the new seedlings. They draw on the nutrients that the compost provides to grow stronger, healthier, and full of goodness for those of us who will eat them.

We cannot survive without food, we have survived on even very poor-quality food, previous generations and current communities are testimony to that but the better the quality of our food the better our health will be.

On a spiritual level, we can also survive on poor spiritual food. This is what happens when church leaders get off the track and do not preach strictly to the word of God. One of the advantages of our current internet services is that if we are not getting good spiritual food at home, we can hunt it down through that facility.

On a personal level isn't it wonderful how God will take my life, something that is not really worth a lot as a sinner and transform me into something that will feed and encourage those around me. *"Wherefore comfort yourselves together, and edify one another, even as also ye do."*
1 Thessalonians 5:11

Oh Lord, may I be someone today that will enrich the lives of those around me and not just trash that gets in the way.

91. Treasure

I treasure memories of my mother's love, care, and common sense. A picture that comes to mind is that one that was shared around the world of two princes running to their mother (Princess Diana) on the royal yacht after they had been separated because their parents had to carry out royal duties.

Many of my own family have had some bad weeks, six months on from the death of my mother. Work, illness, and stress drain the resources of all humans. One missed her birthday card, and another found the one that was sent to her daughter last year unopened. I even dreamt that she hadn't died at all and surprised me with a visit. I asked her if she wanted her jewellery back. During all of these bad days, we all would have loved to run just into her arms for one more cuddle and some common-sense advice.

In the light of the day, I realise that the reality is that she has been taken home to heaven and I can only draw on all those conversations that we had over the years. Yes, one day I will run into her arms again and the arms of Jesus will be there also. In the meantime, I have to rest in Him and listen to his voice.

Matthew 11:30 *"Come unto me, all ye that labour and are heavy laden, and I will give you rest. Take my yoke upon you, and learn of me; for I am meek and lowly in heart: and ye shall find rest unto your souls. For my yoke is easy, and my burden is light."*

During bad days it is hard to remember where our help really comes from. Lord, please help me to remember that my greatest treasure is where the safest arms are, yours.

72. Trivialising Job

As I thought about Job one morning, I thought about how I read his story and think that all his problems happened in a short space of time. My own struggles went on for years and years and there were times when I didn't think I would ever see good times again. Yes, I reasoned, Job had it tough, but it didn't last as long as my tough times seem too and look at all the blessings that he received after it was all over.

But... I thought more and more about this I realised that the trials he faced probably happened over many years, just like mine and by thinking that it all happened quickly, I was trivialising not only the problems he faced but also his commitment to his God.

Even though we are here on earth for such a short period of time we are not in a sprint we are in a marathon, not even a half marathon but a full, long extended one.

There are going to be days when we have to keep going through the pain, we have to keep pushing on, feeling like we are not going to make it to the end. We will hear those voices in the crowd saying: "GIVE UP", "THIS IS TOO HARD", "YOU DESERVE BETTER THAN THIS" and you will think seriously about doing just that. You are human, you are not superman, you are flesh and blood with limits as to what you can do.

Yet... There is JESUS, He is right beside you, He will hold your hand if you let Him, He won't force His help upon you, if you think you can do this on your own, He will let you!

But... He is right there, right beside you, ready, willing and able not only to hold your hand and help you but to pick you up and carry you until you get your breath back, then He will put you down again and let you use those amazing feet, that God gave you to use for Him.

God has put us in a particular place, at a particular time, for a particular reason, He knows why and who we are to help by being there. God is sovereign, we are His creation and all He asks is that we trust Him, love Him and He will do the rest.

"I can do all things through Christ which strengtheneth me. Notwithstanding ye have well done, that ye did communicate with my affliction." Philippians 4:13-14.

73. Twisted and Toughened

I saw a beautiful picture of a tree that had been twisted and toughened over time. You cannot help but wonder what storms it had endured to get to this state. Endured it has and while it is now dead, it is still a thing of beauty that gives us pleasure to look at.

As humans, we have to survive storms as well. We get battered by our circumstances, other people, and illness. Nobody comes through the battles of life unscathed. BUT - Do we come out the other side, just twisted and toughened with no beauty? Are we so twisted with revenge, anger or hate that we drive all those around us away or do something worse? Are we so toughened that we fail to show empathy or sympathy for our fellow man and stop caring for those who are going through battles of their own?

It is possible to come through all these things, twisted, toughened and yet still beautiful. We can be twisted with passion to help others, tough enough to keep pushing on when others tell us to give up and by showing a caring spirit, we became beautiful to those that we touch.

One example that comes to mind is William Wilberforce. How he battled all those years, not only to achieve the abolition of slavery, but many other reforms. Yes, he is dead now, but his life is looked upon as something strong, tough, and beautiful.

In Hebrews 12:5-8 we are told that if we face tough circumstances with Jesus as our friend, He will help us, strengthen us and then one day we will go to Heaven to be with Him. That is why He came to earth. When we are gone, will we be seen as; beautiful, twisted, toughened or all three?

14. UP

"Can you get up please Uncle Alex I want to play chess?" This was my granddaughter's request at 7.00 am one morning. The issue here was that her Uncle works night shift and seven in the morning is just too early for him to arise. After distracting her for about an hour he did rise to the occasion as all good uncles do. The other thing that I had to work out was why she wanted to play chess; I really didn't think that she, at age 6, would know how to play that particular game. It took me a little while to realise that she was actually asking to have a game of "pool" or billiards.

I see both these things in myself. My reluctance to get out of my comfortable spiritual bed and do what God wants me to do. How easy is it to stay within my comfort zone and not step up to a new challenge? I'm not quite as good as Abram was at picking up stumps and moving forward. *"Now the LORD had said unto Abram, Get thee out of thy country, and from thy kindred, and from thy father's house, unto a land that I will shew thee:"* Genesis 12:1.

The other thing that I find myself doing is asking God for things that I really don't know what I'm asking for. It's just as well the Holy Spirit knows what I need and can interpret for me. *"Likewise, the Spirit also helpeth our infirmities: for we know not what we should pray for as we ought: but the Spirit itself maketh intercession for us with groanings which cannot be uttered."* Romans 8:26.

God loves us enough to keep prompting us to move out of our comfort zone and He also knows before we do what we are asking, which is a very good thing indeed.

15. Upside-Down

I was watching my grandson play with his toys. He was holding them upside-down in order to pretend they were diving into water. As I watched him, I was reminded of how we have to be upside-down when we dive into real water. I'm not an athletic sort of person and since I'm a little bit afraid of heights, diving was never something I pursued with any enthusiasm. When we are diving, we need to line up properly, push off with some force and plunge over the edge of the diving board. We will never be able to reach the water if we hang on to the diving board for dear life.

As I thought about this, I was aware that there are many times when our lives feel like everything is upside-down. You know, those times when nothing seems to be going right and we are having trouble even thinking straight, because we have so many different issues coming at us all at once.

Some people are very capable of walking to the end of any board and diving beautifully into the abyss below. But some of us (I'm sure I'm not the only one) need to have support and encouragement, not only to get to the end but to be able to dive headlong into the depths of what God has for us.

So, sometimes when things feel as if they are upside-down, I wonder if it isn't God holding us there, helping us to dive into a new venture or area of our lives. When we land, it will not be pretend. It will be very real, and God will be there with us all the way.

"lo, I am with you alway, even unto the end of the world. Amen."
Matthew 28:20b.

96. Want

Where do I start? I could give you a list that might even fill this page but wants are very different to needs. *"But my God shall supply all your needs according to his riches in glory by Christ Jesus."* Philippians 4:19

I sometimes would like to have more money, but then I would probably waste it. I want my house to be finished but then it could get destroyed by storm or fire. I might even want my books to be best sellers but then I might have to cope with much more attention than I really want. I have often wanted a stress-free life but then I wouldn't have learnt nearly as much as have. I could wish for a garden that has no weeds but then how would I get my exercise. I might even want to live on the mountain tops for my entire life but then I would miss the beauty of the valley shadows. I occasionally want to have spiritual gifts that would enable me to answer questions quickly and smartly. If I am honest though my greatest want would be to have a face to face conversation with my mother and to have her arms around me again. That is, one want that is just not going to happen until I join her in Heaven. I still miss her love, wisdom, and care.

"And though I have the gift of prophecy, and understand all mysteries, and all knowledge; and though I have all faith, so that I could remove mountains, and have not charity, I am nothing." 1 Corinthians 13:2

97. Weather

We listen to the weather report every night. We believe what they tell us, well we used to, but they seem to get it wrong more often than not. When I woke up this morning, I found that the clouds were laying very heavily on the ground. My thoughts returned to last night's broadcast with its clear sky and sunshine icons above our town. As I watched the sky, I couldn't imagine that we were going to see any of that promised sunshine for the whole day.

Of course, there were moments when the sun broke through the clouds. I hung out the washing with little hope of it getting dry. I even ventured outside to do some cleaning up in preparation for an upcoming function. All the time I kept thinking about the unreliability of the weather bureau. They just don't seem to have a clue about the weather and what it might do.

It has occurred to me over the last few months that we have put far too much faith in our weather reporters. Just because the pictures from space tell us that the clouds are coming and the computer models tell us that we are going to get a certain amount of rain from the same clouds, does not make it right. Why, because the satellites and computers do not control the clouds or the rain. God does!

When it comes to weather prediction, I often think of the passage in the Bible where mankind had decided that they could build a tower that would reach to the heavens. Genesis 11:1-10 and how God put a stop to their pride. I sometimes think that is what God does with the weather. When humans are so sure that they know what is going to happen, He deals with our pride by doing something different.

98. Weekends

Weekends are, for many, non-existent. As farmers, in particular, will attest to, especially in droughts, weekends mean that the stock still need to be fed, dams need to be checked, stock pulled out of the mud and cows milked if you live on a dairy. This is the way it has always been for those in the Farming industry.

As a working mother with young children, weekends allowed me to catch up on those jobs that had dropped down the priority list such as extra washing, getting children to clean rooms and running children to sporting events.

For shift workers, weekends often mean working and the number of occupations being converted to this seems to be increasing. A few years ago, no one would ever imagine retail staff working shifts. For hospital staff, police and ambulance workers, the weekends are a time they dread as their workloads increase dramatically.

When my father was a boy, for most workers weekends only consisted of Saturday afternoon and Sunday. Sunday was the day of rest for almost everyone. It was expected that you would attend church and spend time with your family, it was considered a day of relaxation and worship.

When God created the world, even He rested for a day. (Genesis 2:2-3) The perfection meant that we didn't need to toil, but once this was broken, we had to work. This means that time needs to be set aside to rest and worship our God (Exodus 34:21, Exodus 20:9 and Deuteronomy 5:13).

We should worship our Lord every day, regardless of whether we are working or not but we also need to rest from our work and I understand that for working people that day could be any day during the week not just Sunday.

99. What I Wish For

I wish for a mansion, not an earthly one although I must admit that I like looking at those that have been built here. I also have particular tastes when it comes to those available down here. I have a real love for what is called the Queenslander style. It probably has something to do with some deeply buried good memories of staying with my grandparents in Brisbane when I was a small child. Who knows, I don't for sure, but it is there.

When I tell you that I wish for my heavenly mansion, I'm not saying that I want it now. After all, I also hope that I have plenty of work to do for the Lord first but I have just walked through a dark valley this last couple of weeks and that mansion seemed a little closer to me, at times.

This much I do know; when I get to see it, it will be finished, it will be beautiful, in fact, it will be stunning, and it will be mine.

John 14:2-3 says *"In my Father's house are many mansions: if it were not so, I would have told you. I go to prepare a place for you. And if I go and prepare a place for you, I will come again, and receive you unto myself; that where I am, there ye may be also."*

I have recently become aware of just how much we cannot know about what our future is going to hold, simply because we do not have hindsight. We shake our heads at the disciples for their lack of insight but here we are 2000 years later, and things are still happening differently to what they thought it would be. Walking by faith just means that we can speculate but we still accept that: WHAT WILL BE, WILL BE.

100. What I'm Doing Now

I'm sitting in a lovely sunny spot, thinking, writing and being very grateful. I am grateful that my family is safe after a close call yesterday. I'm writing to our local member asking him if there is anything that can be done about that particular intersection, so that another family doesn't have to experience the loss of a loved one there. And... I'm thinking about how it almost always takes a close call for people to start taking action. I have known and hated that corner, yes; I hated it, for many years but I have avoided using that intersection rather than making my concerns known. But.... Now, I nearly lost my granddaughter, and I could have lost my daughter and suddenly I want something done. I ask myself, if someone else's family had been involved yesterday, would I be so determined to be heard?

I look at the table beside me and see the mess it's in and realise that I, in particular, and maybe all of us are too prone, even on a world scale, to let things slide cleaning up fixing the problem before it becomes one. There are a few industries where creating is still going on but on most levels, it seems that we think it's been done or it's someone else's problem.

I have to wonder if there is some level of this thinking in church and at spiritual levels as well - just a thought.

The verse that comes to mind today is: *"How then shall they call on him in whom they have not believed? and how shall they believe in him of whom they have not heard? and how shall they hear without a preacher?"* Romans 10:14.

The question for me is, can I expect any mess to be cleaned up if I do not start by getting involved and doing something, even if it is just a letter to someone with more authority than myself but more importantly I cannot expect the mess in my life to be fixed if I don't go to Jesus and ask Him into my life so that He can start working in it and transforming.

All these titles are available as eBooks

Turning Water into Wine
100 Stories of God's Hand in Life

More Water into Wine
100 Stories of God's Hand in Life

Still More Water into Wine
100 Stories of God's Hand in Life

365 Glasses of Wine
Short Devotionals for each day of the year

Reflections
Australian Stories from my Father's Past

Conversations with Myself – Volume 1
100 Stories of Hope, Faith and Determination

Whispers from on High
Poems and short stories

Follow Helen Brown on:
Facebook: https://www.facebook.com/HelenBrownCollection/

Instagram: https://www.instagram.com/helen_brown_books/

Pinterest: https://www.pinterest.com.au/helenbrown58726/

www.ingramcontent.com/pod-product-compliance
Lightning Source LLC
Chambersburg PA
CBHW030302010526
44107CB00053B/1779